The Ultimate ADHD Workbook for Women

Daily 20-Minute Exercises to Overcome ADHD, Improve Focus, Regulate Your Emotions and Reclaim Your Life

Mikaela Salazar

Copyright © 2025 by Mikaela Salazar

All rights reserved.

No part of this book may be reproduced in any form or by any electronic or mechanical means, including information storage and retrieval systems, without written permission from the author, except for the use of brief quotations in a book review.

Contents

Introduction	v
1. WOMEN WITH ADHD: THE SECRET SUPERHEROES	1
Lifting The Curtain: ADHD Unveiled	2
ADHD In Women, Decoded	4
Your ADHD Superpowers	8
Exercise 1	11
20-Minute Challenges	14
2. RIDING THE EMOTIONAL ROLLERCOASTER	17
When Emotions Run Wild	18
Understanding Emotional Overwhelm	19
Strategies For Emotional Dysregulation	22
Exercise 2	28
20-Minute Challenges	35
3. MASTERING EXECUTIVE FUNCTION AND DAILY ROUTINES	36
What Makes Us Different From Non-ADHDers	37
Strategies For Overcoming Executive Dysfunction	45
Exercise 3	50
20-Minute Challenges	54
4. THE ADHD-SLEEP PARADOX	55
The ADHD-Sleep Connection	56
Strategies For Better Sleep	60
Exercise 4	64
20-Minute Challenges	65
5. DECLUTTERING YOUR SPACE AND MIND	66
Impact of Disorganization on Women	67
Strategies for Overcoming Disorganization	69
Tips on How to Keep a Lid on the Chaos	72
Exercise 5	75
20-Minute Challenge	77
6. NAVIGATING SOCIAL LIFE	79
Exploring the Friendship Equation	80
ADHD and Romantic Relationships	81

Parenting With ADHD	83
Finding Your Tribe: Navigating Relationship Problems	84
Exercise 6	90
20-Minute Challenges	94
7. SURVIVING FINANCIAL THUNDERSTORMS	**96**
Common Financial Challenges	97
ADHD-Friendly Budgeting Techniques	98
Exercise 7	103
20-Minute Challenges	105
8. WHAT'S YOUR DIET GOT TO DO WITH IT?	**106**
The Hidden Link Between ADHD And Nutrition	107
Exploring the ADHD Diet	109
Unraveling Genetic Anomalies	112
ADHD and Heart Rate Variability (HRV)	113
Exercise 8	116
20-Minute Challenges	118
Final Thoughts	119
References	121
About the Author	127

Introduction
My ADHD Journey: From Chaos and Confusion to Self-Love and Acceptance

"Why fit in when you were born to stand out?"

— *Dr. Seuss*

ADHD? Me? I almost laughed out loud.

As a woman on the brink of hitting the Big Four-Oh, I was quick to dismiss the idea. Like so many others, I was under the impression that it was a man's disorder, mostly prevalent during childhood. Women didn't have ADHD, much less a full-grown woman pushing forty. My reaction didn't shock my therapist one bit. She recommended that I undergo a psychiatric assessment and called it a day.

Although I initially balked at the idea, my curiosity eventually got the better of me. What if she was right? What if I had it? Could it be the answer to all my problems?

All this happened five years ago. I barely recognize the person I was back then. My diagnosis altered my life's trajectory. I find it hard to believe I lived with it for so long, without suspecting a thing. In hindsight, I could see the signs. They were always there, as bright as day. I just kept turning a blind eye to them, mistaking them for laziness and wallowing in self-blame.

Introduction

My inability to stay focused and get things done spiraled out of control when I became a mother. At first, I attributed the near-constant brain fog and forgetfulness to my brand-new "mommy brain." The long sleepless nights and constant demands of the baby during the day would affect anyone's ability to function. Oddly enough, my kids grew out of wearing diapers, but my symptoms stayed.

As my family grew, my problems escalated. By the time I had baby number three, I was at my wits' end. With three kids to look after, the list of chores was never-ending. My mind was constantly at work, worrying and fretting about things that needed to be done. The tasks kept piling up. As soon as I took care of one problem, another crisis emerged. Even with my husband's help, I saw myself falling behind, unable to reel in the chaos and get things in order.

Doctors' appointments, dental visits, school meetings, dance recitals, and grocery runs—I was always on the move and never on time. The house always looked like a tornado had passed through it. My emotions were all over the place. Frequent mood swings, bursts of hyperactivity, and long spells of idleness became my norm.

My personal life was a mess, to say the least, and my performance at work was no better. I'd used every excuse under the sun for showing up late. The missed deadlines and careless mistakes no longer surprised my manager. My employer's patience was running thin.

Every time I fell short of fulfilling my role as a caretaker, partner, or employee, my self-esteem took a hit. Eventually, my motivation to get things done hit rock bottom. I went from "I'm-not-very-good-at-this" to "Why-bother-trying?"

The day I finally walked into the therapist's office, ADHD was the last thing on my mind. Just over a year prior to that visit, my eldest son had been diagnosed with ADHD, and I didn't relate to his symptoms at all. Little did I know ADHD has a wide range of symptoms that show up differently in different people.

The journey after my diagnosis was an emotional one. I realized the many ways my symptoms were interfering with my life, and I learned the right tools and techniques for coping with them. When I think about what my life was like before I was diagnosed, I can't help but see all the missed opportunities and setbacks I could've avoided if only I had known how to work with my

Introduction

ADHD brain. Sadly, I know I'm not the only one who feels this way; most women with ADHD are either misdiagnosed or diagnosed as adults.

While ADHD doesn't discriminate by gender, women are less likely to be diagnosed than men. On average, men are diagnosed with ADHD four times more often than women.[1] Gender biases play a significant role in this. Hyperactive young boys are more likely to be identified as having ADHD than young girls, whose symptoms are often dismissed as common female characteristics. *Oh, she just talks too much. She just likes daydreaming. She's just sensitive, that's all.*

The sad reality is that these young girls find it increasingly difficult to cope with their condition as adult women. The roles and responsibilities thrust upon them by society bring their shortcomings to the forefront. Daily challenges of taking care of loved ones, managing their homes and careers, and showing up for their friends and partners take a toll on their mental health, worsening their ADHD symptoms.

It's a struggle I know all too well. For a long time, I let shame, guilt, and self-blame build up around my pending and unfinished tasks, chip away at my confidence, and further hinder my ability to get things done. My inability to focus often caused me to abandon tasks, scrap plans, forget commitments, and ultimately become a social recluse.

Therapy and medication helped ease some of my symptoms, but the real change happened when I decided to take matters into my own hands and develop a deep understanding of my ADHD. Before I knew it, hyperfocus kicked in, and I was knee-deep in research, scouring books, scientific papers, and articles in search of useful strategies. The more I learned, the more I started to value my ADHD brain. I started to see my strengths more than my weaknesses and realized I wasn't insufficient or inadequate—I was simply different.

This change of mindset made me question the lack of support and widespread negative attitudes toward women with ADHD. I may have managed to conquer my symptoms, but what about the millions of other women who didn't have access to therapy or medication? My desire to help others like me compelled me to write this book to pass along the tools and techniques that helped me get my life back on track.

Introduction

This book is a collection of lessons learned, tips, and strategies for overcoming common ADHD challenges. It's a map to help you navigate the ups and downs of being neurodivergent (having a different brain) and unlock your many superpowers. Through this book, you'll discover the reasons behind your eccentricities and effective strategies for leveraging your strengths and overcoming your weaknesses. My goal with this book is to empower you to improve your life and take back control so you can live the life you want to live.

As women with ADHD, we need to embrace and celebrate our differences rather than let society dictate how we live. So many of us remain unaware of the strengths of our wandering minds. We fixate on the problems, ignoring our many unique talents and letting shame accumulate around our failures. While challenging at times, ADHD gives us a unique perspective on the world, spicing up our lives with zest and flavor and enabling us to earn the moniker **_neurospicy_**. This book is a reminder that your ADHD is not a disability that you must hide. It's your secret superpower.

So, let's put on our capes and shatter the stereotypes. It's time to rise above the challenges and live the lives we deserve.

Audiobook Offer

If you love listening to audiobooks on-the-go or would enjoy a narration as you read along, I have great news for you! You can download the audiobook version of **The Ultimate ADHD Workbook for Women** for **FREE** (Regularly $14.95) just by signing up for a **FREE 30-day Audible trial!**

Scan QR codes with camera or go to links below

USA
bit.ly/466oa35

UK
bit.ly/3JEZEyv

CANADA
bit.ly/4nc7Ynw

Chapter 1
Women With ADHD: The Secret Superheroes
Understanding the Signs and Symptoms

"What's the greatest lesson a woman should learn? That since day one, she's already had everything she needs within herself. It's the world that convinced her she did not."

— *Rupi Kaur*

All through my life, I've been trying to shrink myself to fit in and feel accepted. My ADHD made me *too much* everything: too hyper, too loud, too energetic. From a young age, I was made to feel as if something was wrong with me. The constant criticism made me feel like a contortionist at the circus, bending into impossible positions to fit inside a tiny box.

Masking my symptoms came naturally to me. I denied and suppressed the parts of me that made me unique so I could blend in with everyone else. For a while, it worked. My life didn't appear to be falling apart at the seams. I graduated from college with good grades, kept my jobs, and tied the knot with my long-term partner.

Then came motherhood, unleashing the ADHD symptoms I'd carefully kept under a tight lid. Being a mother brought my poor time management and subpar organizational skill into sharp focus. Suddenly, there was nowhere to hide, no way to cover up my mistakes and pretend everything was alright.

A better understanding of my condition helped me learn to work with my ADHD brain by tapping into my unique strengths. Together, let's demystify our neurospicy brains, how they work, and their impact on our lives.

Lifting The Curtain: ADHD Unveiled

Picture a cat in a roomful of laser-pointed, moving dots of light. The cat darts after one zooming point of light after another, tiring itself out. That's pretty much how ADHD brains function. Like a cat chasing after laser lights or a toddler on a sugar rush, our neurospicy minds hop from one thought to another, always on the hunt for the next exciting thing. We need to peel back the layers and find out what's happening underneath.

Brain Chronicles

Attention-deficit hyperactivity disorder (ADHD) is a neurodevelopmental disorder characterized by parts of the ADHD brain being slow to develop and differing from neurotypical (non-ADHD) brains in both structure and function. Most of these differences are concentrated in the frontal lobe, or prefrontal cortex, to be exact.[2] As the cornerstone of executive function (more on that later), this brain region is crucial to a number of tasks, such as maintaining attention, controlling impulses, and regulating emotions.

A 2017 study found that children with ADHD had smaller-sized brains than children without ADHD.[2] That research also discovered that ADHD brains were relatively slower to mature and showed volume differences in various regions. *Volume* refers to the amount of gray matter. Think of gray matter as the brain's hardware store, providing the brain with the necessary equipment to make repairs and keep things in good condition. Another difference is that a person with ADHD generally has a smaller amygdala (more on this in Chapter 2) and a larger hippocampus.[3] These regions of the brain are responsible for generating motivation, memory, and emotional regulation.

These structural and functional differences in ADHD brains are attributable to the presence of specific genes.[3] Because of these differences, those of us with ADHD find it difficult to regulate our attention and emotions, and this difficulty gives rise to common ADHD symptoms.

Take note: These differences are not necessarily indicative of intelligence level. IQs of people with ADHD range widely, from incredibly gifted to ordinary or below average.[4]

Dopamine Diaries

Inhaling the aroma of cookies baking, walking out of a shop with the shoes we've been pining for, delivery of a hot pizza delivered to our doorstep—such moments spur rushes of happiness, all thanks to a tiny chemical in our brains: dopamine. That high we experience after doing something fun or having a great time is dopamine flooding our brains. Dopamine is a neurotransmitter (a brain-signaling molecule) that generates feelings of reward or happiness. Our fluttering attention and curiosity result from this magic ingredient—or lack thereof.

For instance, researchers at the Duke Center for Cognitive Neuroscience in Durham, North Carolina, US, found that people with ADHD showed decreased levels of dopamine in key brain areas.[10] Research funded by the National Institutes of Health in Bethesda, Maryland, US observed pronounced hyperactivity in rats after elimination of the gene responsible for dopamine uptake into brain cells (neurons).[11]

Such research suggests a strong link between ADHD and dopamine deficiency. One reason for this shortage is that ADHD brains contain more dopamine transporters (DAT) than non-ADHD brains. DAT may be thought of as tiny vacuum cleaners that suck up all the dopamine. A higher concentration of DAT in the brain means the dopamine gets hoovered up pretty quickly, causing a decrease in the amount of dopamine inside the ADHD brain, as compared to the non-ADHD brain.[12]

So, what makes this magic molecule—dopamine—so important in the first place? In addition to making us feel good, it regulates our moods, enhances working (short-term) memory, improves attentiveness, and helps us make better decisions. Symptoms of a low supply of dopamine include inattention, impulsivity, and poor decision-making.

The Troublesome Trio

When my son was diagnosed with ADHD at age twelve, six years after my diagnosis, I didn't know there were multiple types of ADHD. I couldn't relate to his ADHD symptoms because they presented differently from mine. I later learned that ADHD symptoms range from moderate to severe, and no two people with the condition have identical symptoms. Hallmark features of ADHD, such as hyperactivity, inattention, and impulsivity, present differently in different people. Based on the symptoms displayed most often, ADHD can be divided into the following three main types.[5]

Inattentive

The leading symptoms of this type of ADHD are inattention and distractibility. Defining characteristics include difficulty remembering details, distractibility, quickly becoming bored, losing essential items, and trouble following directions.

Hyperactive-Impulsive

Prominent symptoms of this ADHD category include impulsivity and hyperactivity. Although people with this type of ADHD may suffer from inattention, it's usually not a stand-out feature. Common behaviors observed in people with hyperactive-impulsive type ADHD include fidgeting, feeling restless, talking constantly, spontaneity, and impatience.

Combined

Some people hit the ADHD jackpot and end up with the worst of both worlds: combined ADHD, which includes both inattentive and hyperactive-impulsive symptoms.

ADHD In Women, Decoded

Who are you more likely to notice in a roomful of people: (1) someone who keeps fidgeting, moving around, being loud and disruptive, or (2) someone who quietly stares out the window, daydreaming?

One of the reasons why ADHD in women slips under the radar is because our symptoms are vastly different from those observed in men. ADHD in men usually presents as the hyperactive-impulsive kind described in (1) above, identified by restlessness, disruptive and impulsive behaviors, and frequent mood swings. Women with ADHD, on the other hand, typically exhibit inattentive symptoms described in (2) above, finding it difficult to focus, pay attention, organize, follow instructions, and remember things.[6]

This doesn't mean women can't have the hyperactive-impulsive type of ADHD; they're generally just a lot better than men at hiding their symptoms, a trait called *masking*. One possible reason for women to hide their symptoms is the greater societal pressure placed on them to fit the docile image attributed to young girls and women.

ADHD symptoms in women are often overlooked due to the prevalence of female stereotypes such as the spacey, chatty, or forgetful woman. Moreover, adult women are frequently misdiagnosed with depression or anxiety instead of ADHD.[6]

Men's Symptoms vs. Women's

Women with ADHD tend to show symptoms of lower self-esteem and higher levels of anxiety, depression, and chronic stress than other women. Men with the condition display more physical aggression, while women show more signs of verbal aggression. In addition, most of the disruptive behaviors seen in men with ADHD are usually absent in women with ADHD.[6] It doesn't help matters that society emphasizes the role of women as caretakers. It's challenging to take care of others when we feel strung out. Unable to fit into the roles assigned to us, our self-esteem plummets, making us feel inadequate or flawed. This is why women with ADHD are far more likely to mask their symptoms, as compared to men.

Then there are the hormones. ADHD symptoms tend to intensify during periods of hormonal fluctuation. Adult women with ADHD generally experience heightened difficulties with organization, focus, and emotional regulation during menstruation, menopause, and pregnancy. This may lead to increased stress, mood swings, forgetfulness, impulsivity, and emotional sensitivity.

Living with ADHD

Living with ADHD is like being perpetually stuck in crisis mode. Those of us with ADHD feel as though we are running a marathon whose finish line moves further away the harder we race toward it. We spend each day averting disaster rather than working toward our goals and dreams. It's not unusual for us to feel stuck and experience a crushing sense of disappointment for failing to reach our potential. We may come up with the best, most creative ideas but fail to turn them into reality.

The constant pressure to be perfect makes us more likely to mask our symptoms instead of getting the help we need. But despite our spending considerable time and effort trying to appear "normal," our ADHD continues to surface in various areas of our lives.

Relationships

In relationships, women with ADHD constantly battle feelings of inadequacy. Maintaining long-term friendships or romantic relationships takes organizational skills, planning, emotional regulation, and a good memory, some or all of which we may lack. We can't show up for others because our own lives are not in order. We may miss the mark with small things that show people we care, such as remembering birthdays and anniversaries, keeping our commitments, and arriving on time. By consistently failing in these areas, we may give others the impression that we don't consider them important.

Social Life

ADHD drains our social batteries quickly. We may find loud social gatherings too overwhelming and avoid them altogether. We may space out while talking to others, making it difficult for us to remember important details and keep the conversation flowing.

Work

At work, our ADHD may make it challenging for us to concentrate on our tasks amid the noise and frequent interruptions. Things may get lost in the clutter on our desks, and we may find it difficult to meet deadlines, keep a check on others, or schedule meetings in a timely fashion.

Home

Disorganized spaces and mountains of clutter are physical manifestations of our ever-busy ADHD minds. Our houses may be stuffed with items we don't need or use—a result of our frequent overspending or impulsive online shopping. Our homes, cars, or offices may overflow with paper clutter. Our bills might be stuffed beneath piles of receipts and forgotten to-do lists, often causing us to fail to pay them on time.

The Mysterious Case of ADHD Misdiagnosis

One of the reasons I doubted having ADHD was because, to me, my symptoms resembled an anxiety disorder. During my research, I realized how common it is to confuse ADHD symptoms in women with other mental health problems, such as anxiety or depression. This confusion is common because ADHD gives rise to numerous additional mental health maladies and other issues,[6] increasing the likelihood of misdiagnosis. ADHD is often confused with the following:

- **Anxiety disorders**, including obsessive-compulsive disorder (OCD) and social anxiety disorder (SAD)
- **Eating disorders** such as bulimia and anorexia
- **Mood disorders**, including depression and bipolar disorder
- **Sleep disorders**

Within the context of ADHD, the disorders listed above are known as *coexisting* or *comorbid* conditions, as they are the offshoots of ADHD and exist alongside it. For instance, ADHDers may overeat out of boredom or impulsivity or for a quick dopamine hit. Similarly, lack of emotional regulation caused by ADHD may make us more susceptible to mood swings, anxiety attacks, and poor sleep hygiene.

Treatment Options

Being evaluated for ADHD at the ripe old age of forty sounded ludicrous to me at first. Despite my initial cynicism, I went along with the idea. Needless to say, the ADHD diagnosis I thought I didn't need and the subsequent treatments proved to be life changing. If you've made it through your life to date without receiving support for your ADHD, you're probably tempted to question what good it would do you to seek help now. Don't let your skepticism hold you back! Medication alone can drastically reduce ADHD symptoms. Pairing medicine with behavioral strategies, therapy, coaching, or holistic remedies, as described below, can bring about a massive, positive change in your life.

- **Behavioral strategies.** Organizational skills and time management techniques can help bring order to your life.
- **Therapy.** Regular sessions with a licensed therapist can help manage depression, anxiety, and mood disorders associated with ADHD.
- **Medication.** Stimulant medications, such as methylphenidate and amphetamines,[7] can help control symptoms by directly introducing more dopamine into the brain. Non-stimulant options increase dopamine levels indirectly. Both types of medication should be physician-prescribed, and the ADHDer who takes them should be carefully monitored for side effects.
- **Holistic remedies.** Diet and nutritional supplements offer a range of benefits that are too immense to be ignored. We'll learn all about them in Chapter 9, so keep reading!

A combination of the above treatments helped me rein in my focus and boost my self-esteem. The improvement I noticed in my symptoms within a few weeks of combined treatment was nothing short of remarkable.

Your ADHD Superpowers

Public discourse around ADHD is often limited to the negatives, with little or no mention of the superpowers that may accompany ADHD. While there's no denying that our wandering ADHD minds present numerous challenges, it's important to instill hope into our minds by shifting the spotlight to the positives. As I mentioned earlier, I don't see my ADHD as a disability to be hidden. Rather, I see it as a *different ability*. Our dopamine-deprived brains, though difficult to work with at times, open us to new ways of looking at the world, ushering in creativity and innovation.

Harnessing the powers of our unique minds is admittedly tricky, but it can be done. The same characteristics that make it difficult for us to focus and pay attention can benefit us in surprising ways. We can maximize the positives and mitigate the negatives with the right techniques. For instance, hyperactivity, which can be frustrating for many ADHDers, may provide us with higher energy levels than non-ADHDers. A 2018 study led by researchers at King's College London, London, UK, found that people with ADHD had higher levels of energy, more frequently sought adventure, and were more likely to challenge traditional norms and values, as compared to non-ADHDers.[8] Under the right circumstances, these attributes can prove invaluable.

Our dopamine-hunting minds are excellent at generating out-of-the-box ideas that can lead to innovation and discovery. Research published in the *Journal of Attention Disorders* in 2017 observed that people with ADHD generated more original ideas than non-ADHDers when competing with others.[9]

And let's not forget hyperfocus—our ability to fixate for an extended period of time on what interests us. Once we ADHDers find skills we feel passionate about, our brains lock into those skills until we've mastered them. Sometimes hyperfocusing on specific tasks may distract us from other, more important ones, but if done right, it can help us master new skills quickly, pay closer attention to details, and become more productive.

In addition to our natural proclivities described above that shape who we are, the journeys we go on after diagnosis enormously impact our personalities, making us more self-aware and self-reliant. Therapy sessions, self-help books, and ADHD coaches offer a number of strategies for curbing our symptoms and regulating our emotions. With regular practice, many of us become adept at identifying our emotional triggers and controlling our reactions. Over time, some of us may even become more skilled at self-regulation than neurotypical individuals.

Nevertheless, our impulsivity and inattention often get us into trouble. Ironically, this builds resilience in the long run as we learn to bounce back from setbacks.

Our novelty-seeking brains also make us prone to taking risks. This can prove immensely beneficial in the right situations, as it makes us more open to new ideas and solutions.

Living with ADHD is a mixed bag of positives and negatives. With the right tools and techniques at our disposal, we can overcome the struggles we face by tapping into our unique superpowers.

In Chapter 2, we'll explore emotional overwhelm and rejection sensitivity, learn the many ways by which these symptoms hold us back from achieving our dreams, and identify strategies for overcoming them. But before we move to the next chapter, let's complete an exercise to explore our individual ADHD symptoms and superpowers (strengths) and their impacts on us.

Exercise 1
ADHD Discovery Journal

This exercise will help you identify which ADHD symptoms you struggle with and how they affect you. By reflecting on your real-life behaviors and personality traits, you'll gain deeper insight into how ADHD manifests in your life, both positively and negatively. So grab a pen and start writing—and don't worry; this won't take too long.

ADHD Symptoms Checklist

Start with a simple checklist to identify your symptoms. Check the symptoms you experience frequently.

- ☐ Difficulty focusing on tasks
- ☐ Procrastination
- ☐ Impulsivity in decisions or speech
- ☐ Forgetfulness
- ☐ Disorganization
- ☐ Restlessness or fidgeting
- ☐ Emotional sensitivity
- ☐ Time management struggles
- ☐ Difficulty remembering instructions
- ☐ Daydreaming
- ☐ Getting bored easily
- ☐ Oversharing
- ☐ Anxiety
- ☐ Low self-esteem

ADHD Strengths Checklist

Now look at some ADHD strengths, which are your superpowers. In the list below, mark the ones that resonate with you the most. You can even add more at the bottom.

- ☐ Creative
- ☐ Good at problem-solving
- ☐ Curious
- ☐ Strong sense of justice
- ☐ Courage to speak up for the right thing
- ☐ Passionate about learning new skills
- ☐ Spontaneous
- ☐ Innovative
- ☐ Able to focus deeply on activities you enjoy
- ☐ Resilient
- ☐ Self-aware/recognize your flaws
- ☐ Self-reliant
- ☐ Self-dependent

Self-Reflection

a. Think about the ADHD symptoms you checked on the list above and their impacts on your life. Reflect on a time when a particular symptom that you checked put you in a challenging situation or made you feel embarrassed. In the space below, write a description of the problem you faced and how it made you feel at that time.

----

b. Now take a moment to reflect on a time when your ADHD was your strength. Maybe you were able to solve a problem with an out-of-the-box solution or ace an exam due to your hyperfocus. Perhaps there was a time when your resilience helped you get back on your feet after a major setback. In the space provided, write a description of the incident and how it made you feel about your ADHD.

----

c. From your ADHD symptoms checklist, choose one symptom you'd like to manage better (time management, organization, emotional regulation, etc.). On the lines below, write down your chosen symptom and describe a specific goal you want to achieve by better managing that symptom. For example, you might write, "I want to get better at time management so I can submit my work on time," or "I want to get better at organization so I won't keep losing important stuff." Then describe how achieving your goal would make you feel.

_____

_____

_____

_____

_____

20-Minute Challenges

"Willpower is what separates us from the animals. It's the capacity to restrain our impulses, resist temptation — do what's right and good for us in the long run, not what we want to do right now."

— Roy Baumeister

Take twenty minutes out of your day to complete the following challenges. See how many you can get done.

- **Practice self-compassion by writing a letter.** Review your responses to a. and c. under the heading *Self-Reflection* above about an ADHD symptom that, at some time in the past, put you in a challenging situation, was a source of embarrassment, or prevented you from achieving an important goal. On a piece of paper or your phone's notes app (whichever you prefer), write a letter to your past self to express understanding of what you experienced and compassion for the distress or other emotion you felt. Write with kindness as you would to a loved one or a friend. For example, you might say, "You're not lazy—your brain just works differently, and that's all right."
- **Release anxiety by reframing negative thoughts.** Write down your negative thoughts or fears about the future. For example, you might write "I can't do this," "I will fail at this," or "I always make mistakes." Beside each negative thought, write a statement that

challenges it. For example, beside "I can't do this," write "I won't know until I try." Reframe each negative thought into a positive or neutral one. For instance, beside "I always make mistakes," you may write, "Mistakes help me learn and improve."

- **Control impulsivity with the 5-4-3-2-1 exercise.** When you feel the need to do something impulsive, notice these fifteen things in the surrounding environment instead of acting on that impulse: Notice five things you can see, four things you can touch, three things you can hear, two things you can smell, and one thing you can taste. This simple exercise will ground you in the present moment, and the time it takes to notice those fifteen things will help you overcome impulsivity.

Your Free Gift Here!

As a way of saying thanks for your purchase, I'm offering this

Inside the Bundle, you will Discover

- **Daily & Weekly Cleaning Schedules**
- **Master Cleaning List**
- **30 Day Clutter Challenge**
- **Deep Cleaning Lists**
- **Daily Planner**
- **...And Much more**

To get instant access just scan with camera below or go to: seleenu.com/adhd-free-gift

SCAN W/YOUR CAMERA TO JOIN

Chapter 2
Riding the Emotional Rollercoaster
Overcoming Emotional Overwhelm and Rejection Sensitivity

"You don't have to control your thoughts. You just have to stop letting them control you."

— Dan Millman

Most neurotypicals can adjust their emotions as easily as turning the volume dial on a stereo. Depending on the situation, they carefully rotate the dial to find just the right setting: loud enough to get their point across but calm enough to prevent the situation from spiraling out of control. This may sound alien to us neurospicy folks. It's almost as if our emotions have minds of their own. There isn't enough time for us to calibrate our responses. Things just happen.

We may blurt out things we later regret, make plans on the spur of the moment, or fly off the handle at minor inconveniences. With ADHD, we feel everything intensely. In the blink of an eye, we can go from 0 to 100. All this is due to emotional dysregulation: the inability to control our emotional responses. It's like having a broken dial.

As a result, we ADHDers feel increased stress in response to some trivial annoyance. A seemingly harmless task, such as a pending work assignment or dishes in the sink, can seem enormous. The overwhelming tide of emotions makes us freeze and avoid the task altogether. The longer we wait to get started, the more emotionally dysregulated we become, which in turn prolongs the delay. It's a vicious cycle we experience all too often.

So let's explore emotional dysregulation and its offshoots in greater detail and discover how to navigate the emotional rollercoaster that is an inherent part of our ADHD.

When Emotions Run Wild

I once snapped at my five-year-old for asking me to open a candy bar. It's not something I'm proud of; it was one of those ugly moments that pointed to a deeper problem—one I wasn't aware of back then. After the moment passed, I was filled with regret and couldn't fathom what made me react this way. Slowly, I traced my outburst to the initial trigger: The car was too hot. The two may seem unrelated, but that's how our ADHD minds work. A mild discomfort can trigger a cascade of thoughts, resulting in a disproportionate response.

That afternoon, I'd lumbered into the hot car with the groceries, vexed about not having anticipated the car heating up while parked. The minor irritation invited a flurry of negative thoughts: *If only I'd taken the time to find a nice spot in the shade or actually bought the sunshade I had considered buying, I wouldn't have to sit in a burning car.* As I reached for the AC, I remembered it was broken. *Why can't I remember to get things fixed?* By the time I rolled into the driveway of my house, I'd worked myself into a temper, and my son ended up bearing the brunt of it.

Emotional dysregulation is difficulty in controlling our emotions when faced with certain triggers. A research study from 2019 found that the inability to self-regulate is a common characteristic across all three types of ADHD (inattentive, hyperactive-compulsive, and combined). As a result, we ADHDers may overreact in situations that do not warrant such responses. As people with ADHD, we experience emotions more intensely than neurotypicals; however, emotional dysregulation isn't limited to sudden outbursts.

Avoiding a task by distracting ourselves with activities such as lying on the couch and mindlessly scrolling through our phones can be a sign of emotional dysregulation. Our environment can also contribute to feelings of overwhelm. Factors such as loud noises, bright lights, and physical discomfort—like feeling hungry or being cold—can intensify our emotions and push us into overwhelm.

Understanding Emotional Overwhelm

Self-regulation is the ability to be aware of one's changing emotional state and manage one's thoughts and reactions. When a neurotypical person self-regulates, it's almost as if a tiny bell goes off in that person's brain in response to a trigger, allowing them to pull the brakes and decide which direction they want to take. People who have mastered this skill are good at responding to stress and other challenges.

So why can't we ADHDers do the same? Why can't we hit the brakes when things start getting too overwhelming so that we can respond more mindfully? A tiny structure inside our brains might hold the key: the amygdala. The amygdala is the brain region that's in charge of the brain's warning system.[14]

Think of your amygdala as your personal bodyguard. When your brain detects a potential threat or danger—such as a car speeding toward you, or, in more primitive times, a wild animal hiding in the bushes—the amygdala springs into action. It scans the scene, assessing the situation. If it senses danger, it pulls the lever that activates our sympathetic nervous system.[14] Another way to look at the amygdala is as a squad of special forces being deployed to neutralize a threat.

The sympathetic nervous system prepares the body for fight, flight, or freeze responses. It signals the adrenal glands, which are located on our kidneys, to release stress hormones such as adrenaline and cortisol into the bloodstream. As a result, heart rate increases, boosting blood flow to vital organs, and blood pressure rises. Breathing becomes shallow and rapid, similar to the way a sprinter breathes just before a race. These changes occur within seconds, enabling us to instinctively react to threats, such as dodging an incoming car or climbing a tree to escape from a dangerous animal.

Once the danger is gone, the amygdala activates the parasympathetic nervous system to take us out of the state of panic and restore calm.[1] This entire process plays a crucial role in keeping us safe and ensuring our survival.

The danger that triggers the amygdala to act doesn't always have to be a physical danger. The threats we face today have evolved significantly since our cave-dwelling ancestors' time. Most of us no longer worry about being attacked by wild animals. However, the amygdala may still respond to modern threats in the same way it did back then. This is especially true for individuals with ADHD. The differences in the structure of ADHDers' amygdalae and the lower dopamine activity in our brains can lead us to remain stuck in a state of flight, fight, or freeze—much like a car without brakes. Our tendency to overthink further complicates this issue.

Overthinking

Our ADHD brains are excellent at generating hundreds of ideas and jumping from one thought to the next. While this comes in handy when tackling a problem that requires creativity or innovation, it can also lead to emotional dysregulation. For people with ADHD, overthinking is an endless cycle of negative thoughts giving rise to self-defeating behaviors.[1]

Dreading tasks, overanalyzing past events, misinterpreting interactions, or worrying about the future are ways our overthinking keeps us stressed. The rapid-fire thinking we experience can lead to difficulties in making decisions, hesitation to start tasks, second-guessing ourselves, ADHD paralysis, and struggles with anxiety or depression.

Particularly difficult tasks might make us wonder, *How am I going to get this done? What will others think of me if I fail? What if I don't get it right?* Eventually, our self-doubt becomes so immense that we freeze. At this point, the wayward amygdala kicks in to reduce our discomfort by creating distance between us and the perceived danger (the task looming over our heads). As a result, we pick up our phones, lie down on the couch, and scroll through social media or find some other way to distract ourselves to make the stress go away.

ADHD Paralysis

Overthinking often intensifies negative feelings such as shame, guilt, and anxiety, leading to ADHD paralysis: a state of mental shutdown when people with ADHD struggle to initiate or finish tasks due to emotional overwhelm.[17] ADHD individuals usually struggle with these three types of paralysis:

- **Mental paralysis.** This type of paralysis results from difficulty organizing one's thoughts. It may lead to brain fog (decreased ability to process information and concentrate) or other symptoms.
- **Task paralysis.** This paralysis involves the struggle to start and complete tasks. It is caused by challenges associated with motivation, prioritization, and emotional dysregulation.
- **Decision paralysis.** This term refers to the difficulty individuals with ADHD experience when making decisions. Our impaired executive function can make choosing between multiple options particularly challenging. This paralysis often intensifies in high-stakes situations, when our decisions carry significant consequences. As a result, feelings of overwhelm may arise, leading to procrastination or avoidance.

The constant noise in ADHDers' heads and the inability to filter our thoughts makes it difficult to respond logically to our emotional triggers. This causes the smallest issues to feel immense, making it harder for us to regulate our emotions.

Rejection Sensitivity Dysphoria (RSD)

When I failed at my first job interview, I felt my life was over. I spent an entire week locked in my room, agonizing over my failure. This was a pattern for me: Every time I faced rejection, a crushing sense of defeat haunted me for weeks. I couldn't stop thinking about it. I'd replay it in my mind, trying to think of what I could have done differently.

Imagine my surprise when I learned that neurotypicals didn't react to rejection in the same obsessive, melodramatic way I did. As it turns out, rejection sensitivity dysphoria (RSD) is a unique feature of ADHD, resulting from our inability to self-regulate. It is described as extreme sensitivity and pain arising from the perception of criticism or rejection by an important person in one's life. It can also emerge in response to falling short or failing to meet others' expectations.

A 2019 study involving 391 children revealed that children with ADHD were more likely than other children to display rejection sensitivity.[18] Similarly, a 2023 study observed 43 young adults with ADHD. The researchers noted that most, if not all, participants reported experiencing symptoms of RSD.[19]

RSD makes us anticipate rejection even when there is no evidence. Consequently, we become hypervigilant to avoid it. People with the condition experience the following symptoms:

- People pleasing those around us
- Avoiding situations where we think is a risk of failure for rejection
- Experiencing sudden emotional outbursts
- Displaying sudden outbursts
- Experiencing low self-esteem and self-doubt

The debilitating fear of failure can keep us from achieving our dreams. We may pass on opportunities because we're terrified of messing up and embarrassing ourselves. RSD limits what we can achieve and keeps us in our comfort zones. Learning to control our thoughts that are attributable to RSD is the only way for us to break free of its effects.

Strategies For Emotional Dysregulation

As women, we must always hold it together. We're seen as the emotional anchors in our families. We're the ones who must help others calm down—the ones the kids run to when they're hurt or sad, our partners' emotional support systems, and the unfazed, responsible adults in our workplaces. We can't afford to let our emotions run awry.

But for us ADHD women, the inability to control our emotions makes us feel inadequate. Our intense responses make it difficult to fulfill our roles as level-headed caregivers. This adds to our shame, shattering our self-esteem. Luckily, our ADHD brains love learning new tricks. Even if self-regulation may not come naturally, there are a number of skills we can learn for keeping our emotions in check.

Breathing Exercises

Breathing is something our body does automatically. It's an activity we rarely think about or make a conscious effort to achieve. The primary role of this essential bodily function is to absorb oxygen into the blood and remove carbon dioxide from it, through the lungs. Notice how your chest rises and falls when you breathe. This rise and fall is the movement of muscles between the ribs and the diaphragm, a dome-shaped muscle located beneath the lungs.

When we're stressed, our breathing pattern changes. We take quick, shallow breaths using our shoulders rather than our diaphragms. This prolongs feelings of anxiety and stress, keeping us stuck in the fight-or-flight mode. Deep breathing helps us hit the brakes on the body's stress response by activating our parasympathetic nervous systems. Mimicking a relaxed breathing pattern helps relieve stress; decrease hyperactivity, anxiety, and anger; and improve concentration.

Deep breathing exercises help us ground ourselves and stop our racing thoughts. It takes us out of autopilot mode, causing us to pause and reflect on our actions instead of reacting to our emotions. Turning our attention to our breathing breaks our chain of thought, bringing us back to the present moment. It allows us to regulate our emotions and work out the next step.

A 2023 research study at Vanderbilt University in the US found that slow breathing can significantly reduce psychological stress in healthy adults.[31] These results corroborate earlier findings reporting the benefits of deep-breathing exercises. For instance, a 2021 study performed by the Ural Federal University in Russia discovered that yoga and breathing exercises can improve attention and focus in children with ADHD.[32]

Practice deep breathing whenever you begin feeling overwhelmed. This simple method of self-regulation can be conducted anywhere and at any time. It requires only three simple steps:

1. Breathe in through your nose while counting to four.
2. Breathe out through your mouth with your lips pursed (like you're blowing a bubble) while counting to eight.
3. Repeat three or four times, or until you feel relaxed.

This simple breathing technique will help you calm down when you feel worried, distracted, or stressed. Enhance your self-regulation skills by practicing this technique whenever you encounter a challenging situation.

Mindfulness Meditation

The practice of mindfulness dates back hundreds of years, with roots in Eastern philosophies, particularly Buddhism, and religions, including Hinduism. It teaches connection to the present moment and acceptance of our thoughts, emotions, and experiences, whether positive or negative.

The practice of mindfulness originated from the Buddhist concept of Sati, a moment-by-moment awareness of the present. The concept can be traced to Buddha himself in the 5th century BCE. It wasn't until the 1970s that this age-old practice made its way into Western society. Since then, extensive research has proven its efficacy in calming troubled minds and boosting mental well-being.

Mindfulness can be described as the human ability to become entirely present and aware of our surroundings, actions, feelings, and thoughts. It helps ground us in the present moment, promotes self-awareness, and takes us out of autopilot mode.

Our ADHD brains have incorrigible wanderlust. Mindfulness meditation helps train our brains to focus on the now, bringing our attention to our thoughts and actions. So instead of letting our sympathetic nervous systems keep us in a chronic state of stress, we can consciously activate our parasympathetic nervous systems to calm down.[20] Instead of reacting to the first thoughts that pop into our heads, we can take a moment to look at our options and decide on the best course of action. Here is a step-by-step guide for practicing mindfulness daily:

1. Find a quiet place and sit in a comfortable chair. Your feet should be flat on the floor, back resting against the chair, hands on your knees with your palms up.
2. Begin the breathing exercise described above, and look around at your environment.
3. Give your complete attention to what you see.
4. Mentally describe what you see in as much detail as you can.
5. When your mind wanders, take note of when that happens, then bring your attention back to mentally describing your surroundings.

6. Take note of the temperature. Is it hot or cold? Does the air feel still, or do you feel a draft?
7. Also be alert to scents. What Do you smell anything? If you do, is it pleasant? Distasteful?
8. Pay attention to sounds. Is it quiet, or do you hear the TV in the other room?
9. Bring your attention to your body. Do you feel the floor's hard surface under your feet and the chair pressing against your back? Does your chair feel comfortable? Is it soft, or solid?
10. Focus on your thoughts. Observe them without judgment. Are they positive, or negative? What emotions do they give rise to? Identify your thoughts and emotions with neutrality, accept them, and say to yourself, "Not now." Bring your attention back to the room and your five senses.

Achieving mindfulness may initially seem difficult, but with regular practice, you'll find yourself improving. It took me a couple of months to get the hang of it. Now it's part of my daily routine. I use this technique several times a day to control my emotions and thoughts. Begin practicing for just five minutes at a time, then slowly work your way up to longer sessions of fifteen minutes or more. Over time, you will gain better control over your mind, which will help you regulate your emotions and react consciously to your problems. You can also use the 5-4-3-2-1 challenge described in Chapter 1 to practice mindfulness on the go whenever you feel intense emotions building up.

Self-Soothing Techniques

Self-soothing strategies are a set of emotional regulation techniques that help us calm down. They offer relief during times of stress or anxiety. Most of us have helped soothe someone close to us at some point during a stressful time. For example, we have all provided comfort to a friend who's distressed or reframed someone's negative thoughts by offering them a different point of view. Being kind to others may feel more natural than practicing self-compassion. Here are some ways you can comfort yourself during challenging times:

- **Imagine talking to a loved one.** Talk to yourself as you would talk with someone you love. Whenever your mind is flooded with

negative self-talk, pause and take a deep breath. Challenge the negative thoughts in your head and try to reframe them. Replace your fears and doubts with words of support and encouragement.
- **Create a list of kind statements.** Make a list of kind, compassionate phrases you can use to help someone else. These include simple statements such as "I'm strong, and I can move past this pain;" "I'm having a hard time, but I'll make it through;" and "I'm doing my best, and that's all that matters." Every time you feel strong emotions—regret, shame, or sadness—welling up, reach for one of these statements, repeat it to yourself, and take deep breaths.
- **Recall a happy memory.** When you find yourself in a triggering situation, take a ten-minute break and find a quiet place. Close your eyes, breathe deeply, and practice mindfulness for a few minutes before turning your thoughts to a time when you felt very happy. Concentrate on the details of that situation. Try to remember exactly all the sights, sounds, and smells you experienced at that moment. Recall how you felt and the thoughts that ran through your mind. Gradually bring yourself back to the present moment.
- **Concentrate on an object you can touch.** When you're feeling overwhelmed, shift your entire attention to one object you can touch. It can be anything—a small toy, even the surface of your desk. Notice how it feels when you touch the object. Take in small details, such as grooves and bumps and variations in color and pattern. The goal of this mindfulness exercise is to silence the noise in your head, detach yourself from your thoughts, and anchor yourself in the present. You can also use an object that provides you a feeling of comfort—perhaps your favorite sweater or scarf—to boost feelings of comfort and calm your emotional overwhelm.

Battling a whirlwind of emotions 24/7 can be extremely draining. Being ostracized for having big feelings or being too sensitive can make us feel ashamed of feeling so intensely. While emotional dysregulation can make us ADHDers quick to become angry, cry easily, or suffer from rejection sensitivity, it also fosters compassion toward others. For instance, people with ADHD have greater justice sensitivity, a heightened awareness of injustice,[21] than other people. We're more likely than others to stand up for what we believe is right and fight for someone we perceive to be the victim of injustice, sparking positive change in our communities.

Controlling our emotions is an ongoing challenge for us adults with ADHD; however, by following the right strategies and practicing regularly, we can reel in our emotions and learn to react consciously.

The lack of self-regulation in people with ADHD is closely tied to our inability to practice executive functioning. The next chapter is all about this important cognitive skill and how it impacts adult women with ADHD.

Exercise 2

The Emotion Reset Plan

This exercise will help you design your personal emotion reset plan. Think of your emotion reset plan as a step-by-step crisis prevention strategy for the next time you experience an upswell of strong emotions. Your emotion reset plan can stop you from acting impulsively and doing or saying something you may regret later. You can also use your plan to break free from ADHD paralysis and avoid delaying important tasks. Take a few minutes to think about the questions and statements below, and write down your responses.

1. *Identify the trigger.* Think of the last time you had an emotional outburst or were unable to attempt a task due to emotional overwhelm. Describe the situation or thought that may have triggered your reaction or inability to act.

----

2. *Map your emotional and behavioral response.* Answer the following questions to identify and map your emotional and behavioral response to the triggering event you have identified.

a. *Thoughts*: Write down the thoughts that crossed your mind following the trigger you identified in 1. above.

_____

_____

_____

_____

_____

_____

_____

b. *Emotions.* List the emotions you felt when your response was triggered.

_____

_____

_____

_____

_____

c. *Physical Sensations.* Describe the physical sensations you experienced in your body (for example, a heavy sensation in your chest, a tightness in your throat, or butterflies in your stomach) when your response was triggered.

----

d. *Behavior.* Write down how you behaved in response to the trigger. Did you take one or more actions? If so, what actions did you take? For example, did you yell, cry, slam the door, or engage in an activity to distract yourself? Or did you disappear into a shell and do nothing?

----

3. Self-reflect. Reflect on your behavior as described in 2.d. Did it make the situation better? Worse?

_____

_____

_____

_____

_____

_____

_____

4. *Prepare for the future by reliving the past*. Using the strategies described in this chapter, revisit the triggering incident addressed in 1. through 3. above, and write down how you could have responded differently. For example, say to yourself, "If could go back to the time I yelled at my son, here's what I'd do differently. I'd take deep breaths after getting into the hot car and make self-soothing statements: 'The car feels hot and uncomfortable, but it'll get better if I roll the windows down.' After leaving the car and stepping inside my cool house, I'd take a few minutes to calm myself by using mindfulness techniques. I'd pause and take a few deep breaths before responding to my child."

See if you can come up with something similar.

_____

_____

_____

5. ***Create an action plan.*** Based on your answer to 4. above, design your step-by-step emotional reset plan. First, complete this sentence: "Next time I feel triggered, I will_____."

Step 1: Pause and notice. Now write down how you'll execute the first step of your action plan set forth in 5. above. That first step is to pause and notice. You can do something as simple as closing your eyes and taking deep breaths, or you may step out of the room for a few minutes to give yourself space.

_____

_____

_____

_____

_____

_____

_____

Step 2: Choose a coping strategy. Decide which coping strategy you will use, and describe it here.

_____

_____

_____

_____

_____

Step 3: Respond consciously. Write down how you will respond consciously the next time you experience the trigger identified in 1. above. For example, write, "I'll take a moment to detach and gather my thoughts," or "I'll make self-soothing statements."

_____

_____

_____

_____

_____

_____

_____

_____

20-Minute Challenges

"When awareness is brought to an emotion, power is brought to your life."

— *Tara Meyer Robson*

- **Name your emotions.** Next time you find yourself in a challenging situation, take twenty minutes to write down the names of your emotions. Beside each emotion, write a line or two to describe what triggered it and how you responded.
- **Practice 3-2-1 cool-down.** When you feel yourself becoming overwhelmed, take three deep breaths, do two stretches (neck, shoulders, and arms), and conduct one mindfulness activity (focus on an object; observe a scene; pay close attention to the music you're listening to and try to identify each instrument being played).
- **Attempt the task you've been avoiding.** Challenge yourself to carry out a task you've been avoiding. Break it down into multiple small steps, set a timer for twenty minutes, and try finishing the task before the timer goes off.

Chapter 3
Mastering Executive Function and Daily Routines
Simple Exercises to Get the Wheels Turning

"You don't have to see the whole staircase. Just take the first step."

— Martin Luther King, Jr.

"It's not that hard."

I must've heard it a million times. My neurotypical (non-ADHD) friends and family members couldn't relate to the problems I faced. They'd see me struggling with time management, organization, and procrastination, then whip out a dozen solutions. If I just did things the way they did, I'd get them done. "See, it's not that hard. If I can do it, then so can you," they'd say, reducing my ADHD symptoms to a single flaw: lack of willpower.

My diagnosis helped shed light on how my ADHD brain made me different from friends and family. I realized the difficulties I faced had little to do with absence of willpower and a lot to do with *executive function*. The word *executive*, as used here, does not pertain to business executives; it pertains to the function of executing, or doing, something. In the ADHD arena, executive function is a group of complex mental processes and cognitive abilities that control the brain's ability to perform goal-directed behavior: planning, organizing, prioritizing, and staying focused.[21] Executive function enables multiple brain regions to work in harmony like a well-tuned orchestra. This helps us stay on time, make decisions, keep our emotions in check, and get things done—all of which we neurospicy folks find challenging.

Once I understood how my brain perceived and interacted with the world, I learned to work my way around my limitations and play by my strengths. Now we can dive into executive function and explore its impact on women with ADHD.

What Makes Us Different From Non-ADHDers

Picture yourself on a running track. Crouching down on the starting line, you wait for the shot to be fired. The moment the starting gun goes off, you lunge and run at full throttle toward the finish line. But what's this? Your track is riddled with obstacles. You look at the other runners; their paths are clear. Midway through the race, an onslaught of hurdles slows you down: time blindness, disorganization, distractions, and emotional dysregulation. There seems to be no end to the obstacles you must overcome. Other people breeze past as you start to lose steam. Panting for breath, you give up and watch as someone else is crowned the winner.

As women with ADHD, why does it seem like the odds are always stacked against us? The answer lies in how our minds work. Unlike the brains of neurotypicals, our brains are like a fireworks show—full of energy, bursting with ideas, ever ready to take risks and explore new possibilities. Now let's delve into some of the differences between neurotypical and neurospicy brains, starting with executive function.

Executive Function: The Missing Opera Conductor

The stage is set, and the orchestra is at the ready with their instruments, waiting for the cue from the opera conductor. They begin, and each flick of the baton, each hand gesture, gives rise to exquisite music. The musicians work in perfect harmony, creating something magical.

What would happen if the opera conductor were to suddenly lose interest in his job?

Picture the tuxedo-clad gentleman yawning wide, moving the baton aimlessly in the air with one hand while scrolling on his phone with the other. Within seconds, the heavenly music turns into a discordant mess as unpleasant as nails scraping a chalkboard. His executive functioning is impaired.

Because executive functioning takes place in the prefrontal cortex and other brain regions affected by ADHD, we ADHDers find it increasingly difficult to plan, organize, and regulate our emotions.[22] A 2020 study published in the journal *BMC Psychiatry* noted greater executive functioning impairments in adults with ADHD.[27] In other words, the opera conductors in our ADHD brains have either fallen asleep or left the building.

Our impaired ability to engage in goal-directed behaviors such as planning, organizing, time management, and emotional regulation is known as *executive dysfunction*.[23] This impairment causes us to struggle to initiate and finish tasks.

ADHD contributes to executive dysfunction by negatively affecting the following six key areas of executive function:

1. **Activation:** setting the stage for attempting a task and getting started; involves organizing materials, making time estimations, and planning
2. **Focus:** keeping your attention locked on the task at hand
3. **Effort:** putting in the effort and staying motivated
4. **Emotion:** overcoming frustration and maintaining a positive outlook
5. **Memory:** remembering the steps the task requires, what's at stake, and why it matters
6. **Action:** practicing self-awareness by resisting impulses and ignoring distractions

Impairment in any of these six areas causes a number of problems in women with ADHD. Below is a closer look at one specific problem, executive dysfunction, and the challenges it presents in our daily lives.

Impact of Executive Dysfunction on Women With ADHD

Gender expectations make executive dysfunction particularly troublesome for women. As caretakers, we women are responsible for managing not only ourselves but also our homes and families. The many hats we wear require executive functioning skills. Inability to fit into society's mold leads to shame and embarrassment, destroying our self-esteem and confidence. Time management, organization, and sustaining focus are some of the executive functioning skills that are significantly negatively impacted in women with ADHD.

Time Management

Time is a mysterious force for those of us with ADHD. It either crawls at a snail's pace or flies like an arrow. We can never keep track of it. If we're meant to be somewhere at 6:00 p.m., our ADHD brains will trick us into thinking we have enough time to lie on the couch and doomscroll until 5:45 a.m. We're always unfashionably late, and we can never keep up with deadlines.

Time blindness is a common symptom of executive dysfunction. Time blindness is a cognitive condition that warps our ability to perceive and manage time.[24] For example, 2023 research reported in the journal *BMC Psychiatry* found adults with ADHD to have significant impairments in the ability to perceive time.[28] This shows that we don't *feel* the passage of time in the same way neurotypicals do. A distant deadline doesn't register on our radar until the last moment. As a result, we're always rushing to get things done.

Here are some ways time blindness manifests in ADHDers' day-to-day lives:

- **Missed appointments and deadlines.** Keeping appointments and meeting deadlines are constant challenges. We may hyperfixate on certain tasks or overestimate how much time we have left to complete a task, resulting in our missing important appointments and deadlines.
- **Overcommitting.** Our inability to accurately predict or estimate the duration of tasks makes us prone to taking on more responsibilities than we can handle. Overestimating our ability to get things done, we unwittingly cram our schedules with numerous commitments.
- **Procrastination.** Our skewed perception of time makes us more likely to give in to distractions and to procrastinate. Before we know it, a deadline is looming large, and we've wasted the whole day.

- **Difficulty switching between tasks.** Unable to feel the passage of time in the way that neurotypicals do, people with ADHD struggle to transition from one task to another. We find it increasingly difficult to shift focus between activities, and we frequently become absorbed in tasks we enjoy the most, even when they are not the most important.

The effects of time blindness trickle into every aspect of our lives. From showing up to work to picking the kids from school to attending doctor's appointments, we find ourselves constantly chasing the clock and failing to keep up.

Organization

Another key executive function affected by ADHD is our *working memory*. Working memory is one of the brain's executive functions. It's an active process that enables us to work with information without losing track of what we're doing and to keep that information in mind while we're doing it. Think about the last time you had to rely on Google Maps® or ask someone to give you directions while you drive. Your working memory made it possible for you to follow those directions and reach your destination. Our brains holds information in working memory long enough for us to record it somewhere, such as when we add someone's phone number to our list of contacts or enter a security code on a login page.[25] Working memory is a form of short-term memory, lasting only a few seconds.

An impaired working memory gives rise to forgetfulness. ADHDers are prone to misplacement of our keys, phones, or wallets; difficulty remembering passwords, names, and other important pieces of information; and difficulty recalling steps and instructions. Our neurospicy brains, in addition to struggling to remember things, also run out of fuel (dopamine) fairly quickly.[2] A decrease in the level of dopamine in the brain causes a sharp drop in motivation, making it difficult for an ADHDer to continue boring or unstimulating tasks such as vacuuming or doing the dishes.

Because organizational skills rely on a good working memory and require loads of motivation, people with ADHD often tend to be disorganized. We may find ourselves jumping between tasks without completing them. Our houses may overflow with clutter, and chores such as laundry may be ignored until we're out of clean clothes! Low reserves of dopamine also tempt our neurospicy brains to constantly seek stimulating activities like scrolling on our phones or binge-watching Netflix®.

As women with ADHD, we may find ourselves waging daily battles against disorganization, and we may struggle to prevent it from crippling our personal and professional lives. In Chapter 5, we'll look at strategies for decluttering our spaces and destressing our minds, so keep reading!

Inability to Focus

The brain's endless hunt for dopamine—the drive to seek behaviors that release dopamine into our reward systems—makes it difficult for ADHD brains to stick to and finish complicated or uninteresting tasks. While organizing the kitchen pantry, we may get distracted by the peeling wallpaper or the broken cupboard and set out to fix those problems and leave the pantry in disarray.

Maintaining your focus on an activity is particularly challenging when the reward for completing that activity seems distant to you, or you find it boring. In such case, your brain starts looking for stimulation elsewhere. Suddenly, you feel the urge to conduct an internet deep dive into an obscure topic like underwater mining, or you take a short break to read a few pages of a book, and your time away from your task quickly turns into an hour.

An ADHDer's inability to focus usually shows up in these three ways:

- starting a task but failing to stay engaged and complete it
- being inundated with thoughts while attempting to complete a task
- hyperfocusing on an activity or issue that is less important than, and perhaps even unrelated to, the task at hand, and wasting hours without realizing it

Our inability to direct or redirect our focus to the task at hand causes a number of problems. We may overlook details or fail to follow instructions. We may also make careless mistakes or feel compelled to abandon the task halfway through. We may find it difficult to think clearly, or we may experience brain fog, in either case impairing our decision making. While reading books or articles, we may catch ourselves reading a sentence over and over without grasping its meaning.

This digital nature of our world means distractions are everywhere, which makes maintaining prolonged focus especially challenging for people with ADHD. When a particular task doesn't give us the dopamine kick we're looking for, all we need to do is to pick up the phone. The prospect of accessing the countless social media apps at our disposal floods our minds with dopamine. We get the reward we're always craving, and the task we were supposed to be doing gets ignored. This explains why so many people with ADHD also struggle with phone or internet addiction.

ADHD and Phone Addiction

Oftentimes, I catch myself scrolling on my phone in the middle of an important task, and I scratch my head. How did this happen? It's almost as if, every few minutes, my hand, of its own accord, reaches for the phone. And before I realize it, I've burned away an hour, laughing at memes and TikTok® reels. That wasted hour is time that would've been better spent working on the urgent report my boss wants me to produce.

There's no denying that smartphones are an essential part of our lives. We can't function without them. Being without a phone is akin to life grinding to a halt. The tiny devices in our pockets help us stay in touch with others, keep track of important dates and appointments, photograph our special moments, and stay informed. Though it's difficult to live without our phones, excessive screen time worsens our ADHD symptoms and erodes our ability to focus.

People with ADHD are more likely than other people to have some form of technology addiction. Be it social media, videogaming, or internet surfing, the allure of instant rewards from using our digital devices is difficult for our dopamine-deficient minds to resist. Moreover, our lack of executive function pushes us to spend more time with our screens. As an example, researchers at Bournemouth University in Poole, England, examined 150 adults for the presence of addictions to various types of technology, including online shopping, social media, and smartphones. The results showed that people with ADHD were more likely than those without ADHD to become addicted to social media and to develop an overdependence on their smartphones.[5] The instant burst of dopamine that our digital devices have to offer makes them hard for ADHDers to resist.

Excessive screen time worsens ADHD symptoms and makes us reach for our devices more and more. The deluge of notifications and distractions on these devices amplifies inattention and hampers focus, leading to increased procrastination and impulsivity. A study involving nearly four thousand Canadian high school students found that increased screen time, such as an escalation in the use of social media, television viewing, and video gaming, was associated with heightened ADHD symptoms. The results suggests that higher screen time may lead to increased impulsivity, which in turn exacerbates ADHD symptoms.

Smartphones offer instant gratification, which makes it harder for people with ADHD, relative to other people, to redirect their attention to less exciting but essential tasks. This may cause us ADHDers to neglect our responsibilities, which intensifies our stress and anxiety over the long run. Although our constant need for stimulation makes it difficult for us to put our phones down and attend to more pressing tasks, there's a lot we can do to overcome technology addiction and reclaim our lives.

Tips on How to Limit Screen Time

Hiding behind our smartphones and letting deadlines pass by, unmet, may provide momentary reprieve but often ends up costing us in the long run. Luckily, there are steps we can take to break the hold technology has on our ADHD brains. Below are some tips to help us limit screen time and attend to more pressing concerns.

- **Set boundaries.** Screen time-tracking and -limiting apps can help you establish boundaries and limit the time spent using your phone by forcing you to wait for a brief period before accessing social media or any other app you turn to unconsciously. The One Sec® app makes you wait a few minutes and encourages you to take a few deep breaths before you access social media so that you can think about why you're reaching for the app in question. This delays your gratification and helps you break the habit of doomscrolling out of boredom. Similar apps include Stay Focused, Freedom, and AppBlock. Most smartphones are equipped with in-built digital well-being settings that set time limits on your use of certain apps or turn on focus mode to restrict access to particular apps. You can also switch your phone to airplane mode or Do Not Disturb while you're tackling important tasks.

- **Create technology-free zones.** In my house, the dinner table is a no-digital-devices zone. No phones or tabs are allowed when the family sits down to eat together. Similarly, I have a reading nook next to the living room where I can unwind with a good book without being distracted by the constant pings of notifications and messages. Making it a habit not to use your phone or other devices in certain areas of your home helps you break your overdependence on them.
- **Use smart hacks.** Sever your brain's dependence on your phone by making it less appealing to use it. Switch your phone to grayscale mode to convert the display to shades of gray, and remove your most frequently used apps from your home screen. Use physical calendars and notebooks to mark important dates and record appointments. Place your phone in another room while you work on an important task. At night, keep your phone out of reach while you're in bed. This will force you to physically get up to turn off the alarm each morning and will prevent aimless, late-night scrolling.
- **Go on a digital detox.** Devote one day each week to a digital detox. Hand your phone over to your partner or family member for safekeeping and spend the next twenty-four hours without it. Substitute healthy habits for time spent on your phone: Go for a walk, reading a book, or do some mindfulness meditation.

Executive dysfunction and the problems it causes for those with ADHD have profound effects on our lives. Structural and functional differences in our brains make these challenges hard for us to avoid. Nevertheless, there's a lot we can do to mitigate the harmful effects of executive dysfunction, as addressed in the section below.

Strategies For Overcoming Executive Dysfunction

Executive dysfunction makes time management, organization, and maintaining focus a constant challenge. However, with the right strategies, we can minimize their negative impact and restore a semblance of normalcy to our lives. Let's consider some strategies that will help us overcome our executive dysfunction challenges.

Chunking

Chunking is a simple organizational technique that helps us break down big, intimidating projects into simple subtasks. It's an excellent tool for organizing our ideas and creating a roadmap to achieve our goals. It involves creating a mind map that outlines the steps we need to take to achieve a particular goal. This technique enables us to think through problems and make detailed plans without losing focus on our target. Grab a pen and draw a large circle in the middle of a blank paper, then follow the steps below to create a map for reaching your end goal.

Step 1. Choose your main goal. Write our main goal inside the circle you just drew. Your goal can be to accomplish any task of your choosing, such as cleaning out the garage, redesigning the patio, or finishing a work project.

Step 2. Write down subtasks. Use your pen to draw lines radiating from the large circle, like rays of the sun. Draw a small circle at the end of each line, and write down a subtask inside each small circle. Subtasks are the steps you must take toward achieving your main goal. These subtasks are each smaller and more manageable than tackling the entire main task at one time. Each requires fewer steps for completion and can be completed in less than an hour, perhaps in only a few minutes. For example, if your main goal is to clean out the garage, subtasks may include sorting the contents into separate boxes.

Step 3. Create smaller subtasks. Break each subtask into even smaller tasks that will take no more than a couple of minutes. You can go further and break these smaller subtasks into even smaller actions. Draw lines radiating from the smaller circles and then draw an even smaller circle on the ends of each those additional lines. Write a smaller subtask inside each of the smallest circles. You can continue adding lines and circles until you can identify no more subtasks. Here's an example. If cleaning the garage is the main goal and a subtask is to sort the contents into boxes, a smaller subtask would be to obtain the boxes; an even smaller subtask would be to label the boxes; and the smallest subtask would be to transfer the contents into the boxes, based on the labels.

Step 4. Assess and delete. Go over each line, or branch, you've drawn and each subtask you've identified inside the circles along that line. Then, assess whether the subtasks on each line align with your main goal. For each task and subtask, ask yourself:

- How much time and effort will it require?
- Will it have a significant impact on the end result?
- Will it bring me closer to achieving my main goal, or will it cause a delay?

Delete all tasks and subtasks that might create unnecessary delays. For example, hold off on the urge to fix the broken lawn mower and the temptation to install a new shelving unit just now. You'll have time to do these tasks once you've finished your main goal (cleaning the garage).

Step 5. Create the final map

Once you've pared down the tasks to the ones that add value and push you toward your goal, you can move on to creating the final version of your roadmap. This will be the map you'll refer to while attempting to complete the task. You'll begin with the smallest subtasks, complete them, then move on to the next-smallest subtasks, and continue until you've reached your main goal by conquering it one subtask at a time.

Tips on How to Improve Time Management

As previously stated, our ADHD brains don't feel the passage of time the way neurotypicals do. We don't hear the clock ticking toward the required date of completion or dwell on the decreasing amount of time left for accomplishing the task. For us, panic kicks in at the very last moment, when it's too late to even think of finishing on time. ADHD makes us time blind, but this doesn't mean we're doomed to forever show up late and miss due dates and deadlines.

There are numerous tips and tricks we can use to befriend the ticking clock. Listed below are some tricks we can employ to *see* and *feel* time more accurately.

- **Use a timer.** Have you ever convinced yourself a particular task will take only a few minutes, only to find it takes a lot longer? ADHD skews our ability to estimate how long it may take us to finish a certain task.[29] The best way to counter this is to identify the time required for that task by using a timer. Let's say you keep running late for work in the mornings. Using a kitchen timer or the timer on your phone, record the time you spend on each task you perform on a typical weekday morning from the time you wake up until the time you arrive at work. When you review all the tasks and times you've recorded, you'll have a good idea of which task takes up the most time each morning. You can then take steps to shorten that task's duration. For example, if you spend a lot of time choosing what to wear to work, you can select and lay out your clothes the night before. If you dawdle while making breakfast, you can prep the night before by making pancake batter, cutting fruit, or preparing egg muffins and storing them in the fridge. You can also use a timer to keep track of the tasks you most enjoy, so the hours don't fly by unnoticed while you're stuck in hyperfocus, making you late for work.
- **Set alarms.** Alarms are not just for getting yourself out of bed in the morning! You can set an alarm to sound every three hours throughout the day to make you aware of the passage of time. You can also set alarms on your phone for important dates and appointments. For mornings, I set two alarms, spaced five or ten minutes apart, to wake me up and a third for ten minutes before it's time for me to leave the house. All this may sound like a lot, but if you struggle with severe time blindness as I do, it helps give you a sense of how much time has passed and how much remains.
- **Divide time into blocks.** Divide the day into blocks of one or two hours. Dedicate each block of time to a specific task. For example, you might block 10 a.m. to 11 a.m. for cleaning the house, 11 a.m. to noon for organizing the closet, and so on. You can use the same technique to organize work flow (e.g., 9 a.m. to 10 a.m. for

checking emails and 10 a.m. to 11 a.m. for attending meetings). You can use an alarm to signal the end of a particular block or use a time blocking app like the Todoist®.

- **Use time buffers.** Compensate for unseen interruptions or delays by incorporating a time buffer—an extra hour or two--into your schedule. If you need to be somewhere at 8 p.m., set a deadline for 7 p.m., and plan the rest of your day accordingly. But since self-discipline isn't our strong suit, ask a friend, family member, or your partner to check in on you a few hours before it's time for you to leave. Something as simple as a text, a knock on your bedroom door, or a tap on the shoulder can remind you how much time has elapsed and get you moving.

Strategies for Combatting Lack of Focus

"Focus! Focus!" I used to say to myself over and over, as if casting a spell, to keep my mind from drifting, but to no avail. Getting our ADHD minds to focus on a task that we find excruciatingly boring or uninteresting is like trying to nail jelly to the wall. The upside is that there are ways to control our flighty brains. Read on for some strategies we can follow to keep ourselves focused on boring but important tasks until they're completed and crossed off our to-do lists.

- **Fidgeting.** Small, repetitive movements like tapping a foot or jiggling a leg help people with ADHD focus better. A 2013 study discovered that purposeful fidgeting could increase the release of dopamine, improving focus.[30] A fidget toy, a beaded bracelet on your wrist, a stress ball, or a smooth rock you can fiddle with in your pocket can help you self-regulate and stay focused.
- **Pomodoro Technique®.** Instead of focusing on a task for an extended period, break it into multiple subtasks, each called a *pomodoro*, that can be easily accomplished in twenty-five minutes each. This makes big tasks seem less overwhelming and makes it easier for you to focus on completing them. At the end of the twenty-five-minute stretch, reward yourself with a five-minute movement break. When you have completed four pomodora, take a longer break of fifteen to thirty minutes to go for a walk, exercise, or even

dance to break the monotony and reward your ADHD brain with the stimulation it needs.
- **Body doubling.** As people with ADHD, we need external motivators and a sense of accountability to get things done. Having someone working alongside us can drastically improve our focus. This strategy, called body doubling, involves asking a friend, family member, or colleague to work alongside you, either physically or virtually, while you attempt a task that requires prolonged focus. Simply having the other person nearby can keep our attention from drifting. We can also ask the other person to check in on our progress at regular intervals, creating a sense of urgency to complete the work.

For women with ADHD, every day feels like a battle against our untamed minds. Lacking executive function skills makes organization, time management, and sustained focus daily struggles. If left unchecked, these problems can easily cripple our professional and personal lives. Fortunately, there are ways to prevent chaos from reigning supreme. Incorporating the strategies described above into our everyday lives can help us beat challenges arising from executive dysfunction.

While it may sound counterintuitive, sometimes the best way to overcome ADHD-related problems is to hit the snooze button and get a good night's rest. The next chapter will explore how good sleep hygiene can help curb symptoms, lift brain fog, and transform our lives.

Exercise 3

Design Your Perfect Daily Routine

By establishing a daily routine, we can train our ADHD minds to stay focused, finish uninteresting tasks, and remain calm. Planning the day in advance allows us to manage our time better and overcome procrastination. Below, you'll find a template for designing your daily routine that you can adjust and customize to your needs. Here are some key strategies you should keep in mind as you design your routine:

- **Use time blocking.** Divide your day into short chunks of time ranging from thirty to sixty minutes to prevent overwhelm and stay focused.
- **Schedule movement breaks.** Schedule five- to ten-minute breaks between long activities to boost dopamine by physically moving around.
- **Use external reminders.** Rely on alarms, timers, and visual cues to keep you on track.

With the above strategies in mind, let's get started. Follow the instructions below and fill out the template to create your perfect daily routine.

1. List your high-priority tasks that are urgent and important and have with looming deadlines.

_____

_____

_____

_____

_____

_____

_____

2. Now list your important but less urgent tasks. The deadlines for these tasks are not immediate.

_____

_____

_____

_____

_____

_____

_____

3. Make a list of your tasks that are neither important nor urgent and can wait, such as finishing your favorite book or playing a video game. You can get around to these tasks after crossing more important ones off your to-do list.

_____

_____

_____

_____

_____

_____

_____

_____

4. Fill in the first page of the template below. First, enter the day, month, and date for tomorrow or another day in the near future in the blanks provided. Then, under the **Top Priorities** heading, list all the tasks you identified in 1. and 2. above that you need to do that day. List them in order of their level of urgency and importance, from highest to lowest. Under the **Reward** heading, describe the reward you will give yourself if you complete all the tasks on your list on that date.

Day of the week _____   **Month**_____   **Date** _____

Top Priorities

Reward

The Ultimate ADHD Workbook for Women

Time	Activity
Wake Up	
7:00 a.m.	
8:00 a.m.	
Mid-Morning Focus Block Tip: Tackle high-priority tasks during this time.	
9:00 a.m.	
10:00 a.m.	
11:00 a.m.	
Lunch and Recharge Break Tip: Engage in physical activity to get a dopamine refill.	
Noon	
1:00 p.m.	
Late-Afternoon Focus Block Tip: Perform low-effort tasks.	
2:00 p.m.	
3:00 p.m.	
4:00 p.m.	
5:00 p.m.	
Evening Wind-Down Tip: Engage in relaxing activities to transition into a restful night's sleep.	
6:00 p.m.	
7:00 p.m.	
8:00 p.m.	
9:00 p.m.	
Bedtime Routine	
10:00 p.m.	
11:00 p.m.	

20-Minute Challenges

"You'll never change your life until you change something you do daily. The secret of your success is found in your daily routine."

— *John C. Maxwell*

- **Divide big tasks into chunks.** Think of a task you've been avoiding lately. Spend twenty minutes breaking that task into multiple small steps. Brain dump whatever comes to mind, in no particular order.
- **Organize into subtasks.** Arrange the tasks above into subtasks, using the steps outlined in this chapter under the heading **Chunking**.
- **Use the Pomodoro Method.** Pick a subtask, set the timer for twenty minutes, and challenge yourself to get that task done.

Chapter 4
The ADHD-Sleep Paradox
Lifting Brain Fog and Improving Health by Sleeping Well

"Sleep is that golden chain that ties health and our bodies together."

— Thomas Dekke

It's late at night. I'm lying in my bed, exhausted. My body needs rest, but I can't get my mind to stop thinking. My racing thoughts keep me up late into the night. As a result, I wake up the next morning feeling tired and grumpy.

Up until a few years ago, lack of sleep had become the norm for me. I had three small kids; late-night bottle feedings and trips to the bathroom were inevitable, making sleep a luxury. Eventually, the kids outgrew the bottles and the need for bathroom supervision, but a restful night's sleep remained out of my reach.

A whirlwind of thoughts would occupy my mind the moment my head touched the pillow, making it impossible for me to sleep. To silence the noise in my head, I'd grab my phone and scroll through social media, hoping to tire myself out. The endless reels and memes did little to lull me to sleep. By the time I'd put the phone away, the sun would be rising above the horizon. Moments later, the alarm would go off, and I'd have to drag myself out of bed and spend the entire day battling brain fog and sleepiness.

Then that night, I'd do it all over again.

Sleep problems are extremely common in people with ADHD. An estimated 25–50 percent of people with the condition experience sleep disorders such as insomnia.[33] What's interesting is that ADHD symptoms contribute to sleep disruptions, which in turn exacerbate ADHD symptoms, creating the ADHD-sleep paradox. This relationship and how we can escape this cycle are explored below.

The ADHD-Sleep Connection

You're lying in bed after a long day, but you just can't get your mind to stop thinking. Your racing thoughts keep you up even when your body craves rest. If you have ADHD and regularly struggle with poor sleep, then there's a good chance the two problems are related.

Disruptive sleep patterns usually emerge in people with ADHD during puberty and exacerbate with age. Some studies report that children with ADHD experience interrupted sleep due to more nightmares.[34] Adults with ADHD struggle with shorter sleep times, difficulties falling asleep, and staying asleep.

People with mostly inattentive symptoms are more likely to delay bedtime, while those whose symptoms lean more toward hyperactive-impulsive tend to suffer from insomnia. Meanwhile, those with the combined type of ADHD struggle to go to bed early as well as suffer from poor sleep quality.[34]

What Keeps Us Awake?

For most people, there's no mystery to falling asleep. It's a pretty simple and straightforward process. Sadly, this isn't the case for a number of adults with ADHD. Before we investigate what keeps us awake, we must understand how we fall asleep.

On average, humans spend one-quarter to one-third of their lives sleeping.[35] We doze off because of a series of biological and physiological changes that take place inside our bodies during a twenty-four-hour cycle. These include the release of the hormone melatonin, fluctuations in body temperature, and sleep-related movements. These and other mental, physical, and behavioral changes are referred to collectively as circadian rhythms. Circadian rhythms, which control not only the sleep-wake cycle but also hormone release, appetite, mood, and alertness, are brought about by the body's biological clock, which responds to light cues.[34]

Here's how it works. When the amount of light in your surroundings changes, your biological clock detects the change and responds by either ramping up or slowing down the body's production of melatonin, the hormone that helps you fall asleep. An increase in your level of melatonin puts you in a calm state. Your thoughts start slowing down, and your body relaxes. These changes promote sleep, and before you know it, you drift off to dreamland. Your body switches melatonin production on at night, when light decreases, and turns it off in the morning, when it senses an increase in light. Interestingly, people who have complete blindness often have trouble sleeping because they're unable to respond to light cues.

It is estimated that almost 75 percent of adults with ADHD have a delayed circadian rhythm,[36] which means their bodies release melatonin later than they should. Numerous studies have observed differences in melatonin release patterns, delayed production of melatonin, and altered circadian rhythms in ADHD individuals. Most notably, 2009 research involving 182 participants with ADHD and 117 without ADHD discovered that adults with ADHD went to bed later, took longer to fall asleep, and experienced daytime drowsiness.[43]

If you have a delayed circadian rhythm, the biological changes required for you to sleep occur an hour or so later at night than they should. Delayed onset of the changes that induce drowsiness and create the right condition for a restful night's sleep keeps you awake during the night and sleepy during the day.

Common Sleep Problems

With executive dysfunction, emotional dysregulation, hyperactivity, inattention, and inability to focus, people with ADHD have their work cut out for them. Add sleep deprivation to the mix, and facing the aforementioned problems becomes twice as hard. Clocking enough hours of sleep at night may seem to be the obvious solution, but it isn't an easy task for people with ADHD. Some sleep problems we ADHDers face include the following:

1. **Trouble falling asleep.** We struggle to shut off our minds at bedtime, making it difficult for us to fall asleep. It's common for us to experience energy spikes during the night, which may allow us to hyperfocus on tasks we enjoy but usually leaves us feeling tired and sleepy throughout the next day. As we lie down to sleep, our thoughts may jump from one thought to the other, keeping us stuck in a state of mental restlessness.
2. **Restless sleep.** When we finally manage to doze off, we experience restlessness. We may toss and turn throughout the night and wake up tired and groggy the next morning.
3. **Difficulty waking up.** Non-refreshing, restless sleep makes it difficult for us to wake up in the morning. We may display increased irritability and aggression and may resist waking up.
4. **Insomnia.** In many cases, sleep deprivation gives way to insomnia.
5. **Restless leg syndrome.** Restless Leg Syndrome (RLS), a condition characterized by an uncomfortable feeling in the legs that causes a strong urge to move them, is commonly experienced by adults with ADHD. For those affected, falling asleep can be difficult. Research has linked RLS to deficiencies in iron and dopamine, which are common in people with ADHD.[34]

The Effect of Poor Sleep on Women

Being night owls can take a toll on our health, as shown by numerous studies showing the significant impact of insufficient sleep on brain function. Good-quality sleep is essential for *neuroplasticity*, which is the brain's ability to adapt and learn new skills. Not getting much-needed shuteye affects our ability to process and retain information. We may experience more trouble remembering things, find it difficult to stay focused, and experience persistent brain fog. Moreover, disruptive sleep patterns make us vulnerable to a number of health risks such as depression, high blood pressure, migraines, and seizures. It may even affect our immunity, increasing our risk of developing illnesses and infections.

Problems stemming from poor sleep affect both genders; however, studies show that the effects are more pronounced in women. It doesn't help matters that women are also more likely than men to suffer from insomnia. According to the CDC, almost 17 percent of women struggle to fall asleep most nights, in comparison to only 12 percent of men.[38] Sleep problems tend to worsen during perimenopause and menopause due to symptoms such as night sweats and hot flashes as well as hormonal fluctuations.

A recent study published in the journal *Diabetes Care* found that getting just six hours of sleep instead of the recommended seven to nine increases the risk of diabetes in women.[39] Moreover, the likelihood of developing these health problems is much higher in women going through menopause. A study published in the journal *Hypertension* found that delaying bedtime by an hour and a half but waking up at the same time in the morning can lead to an increase in blood pressure.[40] The effect was more obvious in women going through menopause.

Lack of sleep in women has also been linked to weight gain and increased appetite. A study found that women were more likely to be overweight than men due to consistent sleep deprivation.[41] In addition to impairing brain function and memory, sleep loss also intensifies emotional dysregulation, exacerbating existing problems with ADHD.

Brain Fog

"Wait, what was I doing?" I used to stop and wonder about this multiple times during the day. I'd drift off in the middle of a conversation, lose my train of thought, and forget what I was doing while doing it. It was as though my mind was cloaked in a perpetual thick fog that clouded my judgment and caused me to make silly mistakes. I had a hard time concentrating on tasks that required prolonged focus, and I kept forgetting things. Suffice it to say that my performance at work and my ability to perform caregiving duties at home took a sharp plunge.

Brain fog makes performing everyday, mundane tasks a challenge. Brain fog is defined as a state of mental confusion that makes it difficult for us to think clearly, make decisions, and remember important details.[42] It's best described as a foggy or hazy sensation in the mind that diminishes our cognitive ability.

Those who experience brain fog may have trouble grasping easy-to-understand concepts, following conversations, articulating their thoughts clearly, and completing tasks involving multiple steps.

Persistent brain fog may cause increased episodes of forgetfulness.[42] Missed appointments, misplaced items, or trouble recalling important information may occur more frequently than usual. Moreover, having a foggy brain makes concentrating and maintaining focus twice as hard.[42] We may notice ourselves zoning out more often, and we may find it difficult to concentrate on tasks even in a distraction-free, quiet environment.

This perpetual mental haze makes decision-making an arduous task. Our foggy minds may struggle to weigh options, analyze situations, and draw conclusions.[42] This makes us feel overwhelmed in difficult situations that require quick thinking.

Brain fog that results from a lack of sleep intensifies ADHD symptoms, which makes maintaining a consistent sleep schedule all the more difficult.[42] This creates a never-ending cycle that feeds on itself and negatively impacts our daytime functioning.

Strategies For Better Sleep

Our buzzing minds may prevent us from getting a good night's rest, but there's a lot we can do to remedy this. Sleep hygiene refers to habits and practices that promote sleep. By practicing better sleep hygiene, we can make sure we clock in enough hours of sleep to feel energized and refreshed the next morning.

A 2023 study found that improving sleep hygiene in children with ADHD not only improved their quality of life, but also helped alleviate ADHD symptoms.[37] Let's explore the perfect ADHD nighttime routine to help you sleep better, feel less tired, and enjoy a calm mind.

The Optimal Nighttime Routine

As people with ADHD, we can't count on the sandman to sneak in through the window and sprinkle magic dust in our eyes to make us fall asleep. The perfect nighttime routine consists of a set of simple rules to boost good sleeping habits and overcome bedtime procrastination. Read on to see what it entails.

Bedtime Prep

Imagine yourself prepping before a sports match, a marathon race, or an intense cardio session. You don't need to do crunches to prepare for bedtime, but you must be just as thorough and consistent. You need to start giving sleep signals to your brain well before you get in bed. Here are some ways to achieve this:

- **Set an alarm.** As chronic procrastinators, we tend to put things off until the last minute. To help us get organized and avoid sacrificing our sleep to meet deadlines, we need hard stops, reinforced by alarms. Make it a habit to stick to a consistent bedtime schedule, and wrap up your daily tasks before the bedtime alarm goes off. Schedule pending tasks for the next day.
- **Exercise.** If you've been skipping going to the gym or ignoring workouts at home, then it's time to restart your exercise routine. Studies have found that just thirty minutes of daily physical activity can improve the quality and duration of sleep. A 2017 study published in the journal *Sleep Science* found daily yoga and aerobic exercise significantly improved sleep quality in women with Type 2 diabetes.[44] So set aside a few minutes each day for moderate exercise to get better sleep at night.
- **Avoid caffeine.** While a cup of freshly brewed coffee in the morning won't hurt, consuming caffeinated drinks in the afternoon or a few hours before bedtime can disrupt nighttime sleep. Data compiled by the Sleep Foundation found that people who regularly drank coffee in the afternoon experienced more sleep problems.[45] Caffeine boosts mental alertness by blocking adenosine receptors in the brain. Adenosine is a chemical that boosts sleep. Produced by the brain while we're awake, adenosine builds up during the day and induces sleep by nightfall. Blocking this process through caffeine consumption allows us to remain alert and vigilant, potentially disrupting sleep. So, keep coffee breaks to a minimum during the afternoon, and avoid caffeine completely before bedtime.

- **Avoid screens.** Another thing to cross off your list before your head hits the pillow is the use of digital devices. Blue light emitted from your phone or laptop screen can disrupt your sleep patterns and keep you up at night. Switch your phone off an hour before you go to bed and avoid scrolling to make yourself fall asleep.
- **De-stress.** Sleep becomes a distant memory when we're stressed out and the day's worries occupy our minds. There are many effective strategies for relieving stress and anxiety before bedtime, including mindfulness meditation, yoga, tai chi, and deep breathing exercises. A recent study published in the journal *JAMA Internal Medicine* investigated the effects of mindfulness meditation on a group of middle-aged and older adults.[46] The results showed that mindfulness meditation could significantly reduce insomnia, depression, and fatigue. This powerful technique, when combined with other stress-relieving methods such as deep breathing and yoga, can help bring a stop to racing thoughts and improve sleep hygiene. If you're just starting out, and mindfulness seems too difficult, then try guided meditation instead. It includes visualizing yourself at a peaceful and calming location. You can easily download these meditations from YouTube® or popular apps like Calm®.

The Sleep Formula

A simple formula for remembering the rules for getting good sleep is the 10-3-2-0 method. Here's how it works:

- **10 hours before bed.** Avoid drinking coffee. Caffeine has an average half-life of five hours, so a steaming cup of coffee around one in the afternoon will stay in your system till six in the evening. If your bedtime is eleven, then avoid coffee in the afternoon.
- **3 hours before bed.** Limit your food intake. You don't have to starve or skip dinner. Simply try to finish your main meal three hours before bed and reach for a light snack to satisfy any hunger pangs afterwards.
- **2 hours before bed.** It's time to unwire and disconnect. Switch off your phone, iPad, and laptop and go offline. Begin preparing for

bedtime. You can have a brief meditation session, practice yoga, or journal to help yourself unwind.
- **0 snoozes.** Make it a habit to wake up at the same time each morning and resist using the snooze function on your alarm. For ADHDers, avoiding the snooze function may prove to be the most difficult of these four steps, but with regular practice, you can go a long way toward ditching the snooze for good. Hitting snooze and sneaking in a few more minutes of sleep may feel tempting, but it can disrupt your sleep-wake cycle. Waking up at the same time every day is just as crucial as maintaining a consistent bedtime. If you find yourself struggling with this step, try placing your phone out of arm's reach or in a different room, with the volume turned up. This will force you to get out of bed to turn it off.

Living with ADHD means having to deal with cluttered spaces. In the next chapter, we'll look at ways to declutter and de-stress. We'll also explore ways to organize and sort items and bring an end to last-minute searches before stepping out the door.

Exercise 4

The Sleep Hygiene Tracker

Daily for one week, use the Sleep Hygiene Tracker below to record your nighttime routine. Fill in the requested information for each night of the week. Challenge yourself to cut out caffeinated drinks before bedtime, and avoid using digital devices in bed. Review your performance at the end of the week, make adjustments where necessary, and start over the next week.

Habits	Mon	Tues	Wed	Thurs	Fri	Sat	Sun
Time you woke up							
Rate how sleepy/alert you felt during the day? 1 Extremely tired/sleepy 2 Somewhat tired/sleepy 3 Alert							
Number of awakenings in the night							
Did you take any day time naps?							
Avoided caffeinated drinks ten hours before bedtime							
Limited food intake three hours before bedtime							
Avoided screens two hours before bedtime							
De-stressing exercises before going to bed (meditation, deep breathing, journaling, etc.)							
Time you went to bed							
How long it took you to fall asleep							
How many hours did you sleep?							

20-Minute Challenges

"Each night, when I go to sleep, I die. And the next morning, when I wake up, I'm reborn."

— Mahatma Gandhi

- **Worry dump.** Before you go to bed, write your thoughts or worries in your journal. Practice self-compassion, and use self-soothing practices and mindfulness meditation to let go of your worries.
- **4-7-8 breathing.** Practice the 4-7-8 breathing method. Inhale, counting to four; hold your breath, counting to seven; and exhale, counting to eight. Repeat several times over the course of twenty minutes.
- **Guided Meditation:** Go on YouTube® and listen to a guided meditation for 15 minutes. Note: This is the only exception to the "no screens before bedtime" rule!

Chapter 5
Decluttering Your Space and Mind
ADHD-Friendly Strategies for Organized Spaces

"Clutter is nothing more than postponed decisions."

— *Barbara Hemphill*

When you have three kids to look after, your organizational skills need to be top-notch, to say the least. From herding them to school in the morning to getting them into bed on time, you need to be on your toes, dodging curveballs and mounting obstacles. It requires razor-sharp time management, bulletproof memory, and tons of energy and motivation.

But even when kids aren't part of the picture, adult women with ADHD bear the brunt of their lack of organization. Society expects us to keep our houses clean and well managed. We have little room to make mistakes at work, and we must maintain an immaculate appearance at all times.

The fear of being ostracized forces us to mask our ADHD symptoms by making excuses, covering up our poor performance, or cutting corners in an effort to get things done at the last moment. Trying to hide our symptoms and projecting a false image of ourselves might help us avoid short-term consequences, but it's not a sustainable option for the long term. Over time, ADHD-related disorganization can wreak havoc on our lives, and we may find ourselves paying a heavy price for unattended clutter and forgotten deadlines.

In chapter 3, we learned how an impaired working memory and dopamine deficiency diminish our ability to get organized. While our ADHD brains make organization a constant challenge, there are a number of strategies we can employ to keep the clutter at bay. In this chapter, we'll explore the impact of disorganization on women and discuss effective strategies for overcoming the chaos. Dive in, and explore how disorganization affects women.

Impact of Disorganization on Women

The house is a mess, the kids are bouncing off the walls, there are dirty dishes in the sink, clothes are spilling from the overstuffed laundry basket, and clutter is everywhere. For years, I fought a silent battle with disorganization, not knowing that it was a symptom of my ADHD.

Chronic disorganization can lead to considerable stress and emotional overwhelm. It creates an environment that worsens ADHD symptoms such as distractibility, inattention, and inability to focus. Living in such an environment can exact a heavy toll on women, contributing to their low self-esteem.

Women with ADHD tend to blame themselves for falling short of society's standards. We let ourselves be defined by our shortcomings and live in constant fear of criticism and rejection. We're more likely to internalize our pain, blaming ourselves for the struggles we face, which can take a toll on our mental health and result in anxiety and depression. Instead of taking pride in standing out, we place the burden on ourselves to fit in and fulfill the roles thrust upon us due to our gender.

A Canadian study on adult women with ADHD found that the participants blamed themselves when undesirable events took place in their lives.[47] This study also showed that women diagnosed later in life showed higher levels of Rejection Sensitivity Dysphoria (RSD). Women in general were found to have a higher tendency than men for self-blame, which leads to frustration, negativity, and self-doubt.

Motherhood

Motherhood demands impeccable organizational skills. Even on our worst days, we mothers must drag ourselves out of bed and get things done so everyone else can stay on their schedules. As women, we're socially conditioned to take on the lion's share of responsibilities when it comes to household chores and parenting, despite our limitations. We often find ourselves jumping through hoops to meet others' expectations and fulfill the roles assigned to us.

Juggling the demands of motherhood with ADHD can be overwhelming and stressful. We may constantly push ourselves to the limit to meet our children's needs, often sacrificing our own in the process. The pressures of being a parent, combined with our low self-esteem and self-doubt, can lead to feelings of guilt, shame, and inadequacy. We may constantly compare ourselves to neurotypical mothers and feel like failures.

It's extremely common for women with ADHD to be diagnosed when their children are diagnosed. This was certainly the case with me. I discovered I had ADHD just over a year after my eldest son was diagnosed. It marked a turning point in my life because it helped me and my family understand the challenges I faced. When we women recognize our ADHD symptoms, it helps us manage them better. It also allows us to get to the root cause of our problems and find solutions.

Masking

Women with ADHD are often experts at concealing their struggles. The criticism we're subjected to when we fall short of meeting the standards set by society compel us to mask our symptoms. *Masking* is an ADHD individual's attempt to present themselves in a way that makes them seem like a neurotypical person. It is estimated that about one-third of people with ADHD try to mask their symptoms.[48]

For example, we may obsessively check our belongings to make sure we don't lose anything. An appointment late in the evening may keep us on edge all day, anxious to avoid showing up late due to our time blindness. We may take excessive notes because we don't trust our memories, or we may focus too intensely on someone's face when listening to them speak, so we won't miss important details. Planning and organizing our days may become an obsession involving the use of multiple color-coding systems and planners to stay on top of our daily schedules.

To emulate our neurotypical counterparts, we take on more responsibilities than we can handle and sacrifice our own mental and physical well-being to get them done. Our desire to feel accepted and avoid being stigmatized pushes us toward perfectionism. When it comes to cleaning and organizing our homes, we may get sidetracked and stop to fix things that don't require our immediate attention. We're prone to biting off more than we can chew and ending up feeling burned out and exhausted.

The behaviors described above are coping strategies that may offer some short-term relief, but they often make managing ADHD symptoms more difficult in the long run. Eventually, the facade is destined to fall apart, forcing us to look our problems in the eye and acknowledge our shortcomings.

Strategies for Overcoming Disorganization

Almost all of us sometimes find ourselves running late or forgetting something important. We all have days when the house is a mess and we're running behind on our plans. But with ADHD, disorganization seeps into every aspect of our lives. It is chronic and pervasive despite our best efforts to become more organized. Even if we do manage to maintain an outward appearance of being calm and orderly, it takes immense effort to keep up the facade that eventually crumbles, exposing our shortcomings.

The key to becoming "well enough" organized in our daily lives is to take up habits that we can maintain easily over the long term. I use the words "well enough" because it's important for us to adopt a more flexible approach. As people with ADHD, we're inclined to take an all-or-nothing approach to organization: Unless we finish all the tasks on our to-do list, our efforts don't count. It's this black-and-white thinking that ultimately becomes our downfall, keeping us perpetually stuck in a cycle of shame and guilt that prevents us from making positive changes in our lives.

We ADHDers need some simple strategies to follow for organizing our homes and office spaces and making them more manageable. It may surprise you how easy it is to do that if we have the right tips and tricks at our disposal.

One Room at a Time

Thinking about a task as a whole may make it appear more daunting than it is. Straightening out the garage, organizing the bedroom closet, or decluttering the junk drawer may seem like an enormous undertaking. But breaking these big tasks into small, achievable steps makes them less intimidating. It also helps us overcome ADHD paralysis and encourages us to get started.

Instead of trying to put the entire house in order, start with just one room. You can break this down further by focusing on just one area of that one room at first. Something that works for me is to clean one room each day of the week. This makes Mondays the day I organize the kitchen, Tuesdays when I tackle the living room, Wednesdays for getting the bedroom in order, and so on. I may not get everything done in a day, but even getting halfway to my goal is enough. Whatever's left can be dealt with in the next cleaning session.

This approach also makes it easier to focus and stay motivated. You simply start by making a list of small, manageable tasks for each day, set the timer, and focus on one task at a time. Here are the steps you need to take to implement this method:

1. Select areas in the room that you want to tidy up.
2. Rank in order of easiest to hardest.
3. Start with the easiest one.
4. Make a list of tasks you'll need to do.
5. Work in sessions ranging from 15 to 60 minutes.
6. Move onto the more difficult areas on your list as you get done with the easier ones.

Remember to give yourself a dopamine refill when a session ends. Reward yourself by doing something you enjoy, such as a few minutes to scroll through your phone, play a video game, or eat a snack. But don't get too carried away with the rewards: set firm limits on reward time so you'll return to your task and pick up where you left off. Offer yourself a more meaningful reward when you hit a big milestone, like getting the entire living room organized.

This reward can be something you thoroughly enjoy, like going to a movie or having dinner at your favorite restaurant.

Sort It Out

One of the biggest challenges I face is getting rid of clutter. I find it so difficult to part with random objects that at one point, my house came uncannily close to resembling an Egyptian tomb. I had it stuffed to the brim with objects I didn't need, like a Pharaoh preparing to enter the afterlife with his most prized possessions. A great way to get out of the habit of hoarding and cut down clutter is to categorize and sort items.

During your weekly organization sessions, you're bound to come across lots of knick-knacks, old clothing, mugs, and so on that have been sitting around for ages and serve no purpose. Sort them into the following categories:

- Keep
- Toss/recycle
- Donate/sell
- Decide later

Get a few plastic bins or boxes and label them with the above categories. Keep these nearby as you clean. If you can't make up your mind about a certain item, toss it in the "Decide later" container. Set a deadline for yourself on your phone or the calendar to go through this container and make a decision about the items inside. A rule that helps me decide which items I should keep or discard goes like this: If I haven't used the item in a year or more, then the chance of it serving a useful purpose any time in the near future is pretty slim, so out it goes.

A Home for Everything You Own

Everything in your house needs a home of its own! Yes, you read that right. Create "homes" for your items by designating a particular area for them. For example, the shoes always go in the shoe cabinet, the keys go on the key holder, the phone goes on the table beside the bed, and your bag on the peg behind the door. Return each item to its designated spot when you return home or after you're done using it.

Returning items to their place, as opposed to putting them down wherever they feel convenient and forgetting about them, can help create a more organized space. It also makes it easier to find things when you're in a rush. Instead of tearing down the house to find your keys or wallet, you simply grab them from their "home" and get going. Remember the age-old organizing mantra: "A place for everything and everything in its place."

Organizing With Kids

If you're a parent with a bunch of young ones running around, you may be wondering how you could possibly apply the tips above. But remember: Your goal is not to achieve perfection. Your goal is to keep your spaces reasonably clean and organized. One way to do so, as a parent, is to get the kids on your team.

This is where my Sunday basket solution comes in handy. It's a strategy I use frequently with my own kids to get them in on the cleaning. Set out a small basket or other container, set the timer for ten minutes, and get the kids to do a speed clean. They have to take turns running through the house, collecting items that are out of place and putting them in the container. The one who picks the most clutter before the timer goes off wins. This game makes the decluttering job a lot easier and builds organizational skills in children.

You can also teach your children the concept of creating a home for their shoes, jackets and school bags and reinforce the idea by offering rewards. Having young kids around makes organization a lot harder to maintain, but it's important to get them to participate in our efforts: The organizational habits they build early on will benefit them as adults. Adding an element of fun and excitement to the process usually does the trick.

Tips on How to Keep a Lid on the Chaos

We've all been there: We go out of our way to clean and organize our homes, only for the mess to return within a few hours or days, at best. Here are some tips on how to keep a lid on the chaos in your home and keep things organized for a long time:

- **Create a launchpad.** Reserve an area close to the door for your most important items you can't leave the house without, like your phone, wallet, and keys. You can also keep a handbag ready by the door, filled with everything you'll need for preventing last-minute searches and to avoid losing those items.
- **Switch to digital options.** Bring an end to the paper pileup by adopting digital options. Pay the bills online and choose electronic receipts whenever possible. Take photos of recipes, receipts, or other papers. You can do the same for your kids' drawings or art projects and keep the memories as photographs while discarding the originals.
- **Less stuff means less chaos.** The best way to prevent clutter from taking over your house is to have less stuff to worry about. Review your spending habits and make a rule for yourself to get rid of one old item when you buy something new. For instance, you can get rid of a piece of clothing you no longer wear each time you buy a new dress or donate your old shoes when you buy a new pair.
- **Create a catch-all bowl.** This is where all your out-of-place items go, including random receipts, notes on scraps of paper, hair ties, and small broken bits and pieces you find lying around. Go through the items while you're watching TV and toss or keep them based on whether you need them or not.
- **Do a two-minute cleanup.** Take two minutes after you've finished an activity, like making coffee, to clean the area you used. This can be something as simple as washing the coffee pot, returning it to its place, and wiping down the counter.
- **Do a quick speed clean.** Use the Sunday Basket solution described earlier in this chapter to do a quick ten- to fifteen-minute clean up twice a day. Get your family to join in and turn it into a competition. Sort through the items in the basket while sipping a refreshing drink and watching YouTube®.

Our neurospicy brains lack the skills required to be naturally organized and keep our spaces well-maintained. Living in disorganized environments bursting with clutter makes it difficult for us to concentrate. It adds stress to our daily lives as we scour through piles of junk for the things we need.

Lacking executive function skills, we need more structure in our lives to meet demands at our workplaces and homes. We need to transform the messy, chaotic spaces into organized ones so we can minimize stress, keep on track of our schedules, and focus on necessary tasks without getting distracted by the clutter.

Fortunately, there are many useful tips, tricks, and habits that we can use to restore order and bring an end to the chaos. While it's tempting to go overboard and try to become meticulously tidy overnight, it's much better to start with small steps that gradually turn into long-lasting habits. The basic tools for maintaining an organized life include making lists, sorting objects, tackling one task at a time, and creating spaces that make it easy to find our essential items.

Now that our homes are sorted and organized, we can move on to another crucial aspect of our lives that ADHD impacts: relationships. In the next chapter, we'll learn what makes navigating social life a challenge for neurospicy women and how we can form better connections.

Exercise 5

The Ten-Minute Declutter Challenge

All it takes is ten minutes! Follow the steps listed below to complete the ten-minute declutter challenge. Once you're done, review your performance, and make plans for your next cleaning spree.

1. In the table below, make a weekly organizing schedule by designating a certain room to be cleaned each day.

Day	Room

2. Choose one room and identify the areas you want to organize inside that room (for example, the bedroom closet, the bedside tables, the TV console, etc.). List those areas in the table below. Based on how time-consuming or complicated the task of organizing an area will be, assign that area a level of difficulty from 1 to 3, using the key below.

    1 : Easy
    2 : Moderate
    3 : Difficult

Areas that Need Organizing in _____ (name of room)	Difficulty Level

3. From the table in 2. above, choose one area to organize, break the task of organizing it into small steps, and list those steps below.

_____

_____

_____

_____

_____

_____

_____

4. Set the timer to ten minutes and start organizing. When the timer goes off, jot down your progress (number of tasks you've achieved) and move on to the next area.

Name of the Area Organized	Number of Tasks Achieved

20-Minute Challenge

"The first step in crafting the life you want is to get rid of everything you don't."

— *Joshua Becker*

- **Do a twenty-minute speed clean.** Grab the Sunday basket and challenge yourself to collect all the mess.
- **Sort and toss:** Sort the items you collected in your Sunday basket and place each in the appropriate Keep, Toss, or Donate container.
- **Review your wardrobe:** Go through your wardrobe and pick five clothing items you want to give away.

Your Free Gift Here!

As a way of saying thanks for your purchase, I'm offering this

Inside the Bundle, you will Discover

- Daily & Weekly Cleaning Schedules
- Master Cleaning List
- 30 Day Clutter Challenge
- Deep Cleaning Lists
- Daily Planner
- …And Much more

To get instant access just scan with camera below or go to: seleenu.com/adhd-free-gift

SCAN W/YOUR CAMERA TO JOIN

Chapter 6
Navigating Social Life
Making Relationships Work and Finding Your Tribe

"Friendship isn't about who you've known the longest. It's about who walked into your life and said, 'I'm here for you' and proved it."

— *Nicholas Sparks*

Growing up, I was the lonely kid in school. For as long as I can remember, I struggled to make friends. I couldn't figure out why my friendships wouldn't last. The problems I faced in my social life persisted well into adulthood. After numerous fleeting relationships, I met my husband, Matt. At first, our relationship seemed destined for an end like my earlier ones. It took considerable patience and understanding on my husband's part to make things work. Of course, I had work to do, too. I had to learn to change my habits and adopt better coping mechanisms for my ADHD symptoms. No matter how hard things got, we didn't give up on each other—and that made all the difference in the end.

Strong social connections are crucial for women who want to lead healthy and satisfying lives. For women who have ADHD, our ADHD gets in the way of forming meaningful connections with others. An eye-opening study at the University of California, Berkeley, in the US observed social relationships in girls with ADHD.[49] That study noted that girls with ADHD faced considerable difficulty forming and maintaining friendships. In particular, girls presenting symptoms of the hyperactive-impulsive type had a harder time making friends. The researchers observed that the hyperactive-impulsive girls were more frequently "rejected" by the girls displaying the shy, inattentive type of ADHD.

Adult women with ADHD also often struggle to make and keep friends. This can lead to significant social distress. This is because women, more so than men, possess a greater need for social acceptance, yearning connectedness with others. Not having deep, meaningful friendships can make women feel isolated and alone.

We need to investigate what makes relationships so tricky for women with ADHD to navigate so that we can learn to lead more fulfilling social lives.

Exploring the Friendship Equation

If we could dissect friendships and examine what they're made of, we'd come across the friendship equation:

$$\text{Friendship} = \text{Proximity} \times (\text{Frequency} + \text{Duration}) \times \text{Intensity}$$

This equation pares friendships down to four core elements. Together, these elements decide how long a friendship will last. Proximity refers to physical closeness, where the more two people find themselves in each other's company, the greater the likelihood they'll become friends. Frequency refers to the frequency of interaction between people. Regular contact increases the chances of becoming friends and building connections with each other. Duration and intensity refer to the length and quality, respectively, of time spent together.

ADHD affects our ability to fulfill the above criteria and form long-lasting and enriching friendships. The challenges associated with our condition make it difficult for us to meet social expectations. Due to executive dysfunction and time blindness, we may have a hard time following through on commitments and showing up on time. This affects how often we see our friends and the quality of the time we spend in their company.

Friendships require us to have good listening skills and pay attention to non-verbal cues. We ADHDers may struggle to listen to others without interrupting, fail to pick up on social cues, and blurt out our thoughts without reservation. Moreover, maintaining friendships requires checking in with others from time to time. Even if not much has happened since the last time friends talked to each other, a simple, "How are you?" can go a long way toward strengthening the connection. Our impaired working memory, coupled with our time blindness, makes us forget how long it's been since we last saw our friend. We may struggle to remember details our friends have shared with us. Additionally, our consistent failure to show up for important events, remember special occasions, and stay in touch can erode our relationships over time.

ADHD and Romantic Relationships

When my husband, Matt, and I started dating, we had no idea what ADHD was or that I had it. He found my hyperfixation with him flattering. My spontaneity and willingness to try new things added spark to our dates. Cut to a few months later, and my frequent emotional outbursts, disorganization, and forgetfulness had him scratching his head. He didn't know people with ADHD often have a hard time connecting with their partners and establishing long-term relationships, due to their symptoms.

ADHD also makes it difficult to form meaningful connections and often leads to misunderstandings between partners. For example, our impulsivity can lead to risky behaviors or rash decisions, causing stress to our partners. We may lose focus in the middle of conversations, giving the impression that we don't care or we're not interested. Our inattention and forgetfulness also make it more likely for us to forget important tasks and fail to deliver on our promises. This places the burden of keeping things organized squarely on the shoulders of our neurotypical partner, which is exhausting for that person in the long run.

Here are three ways our distracted minds affect relationships:

Household Chores and Responsibilities

"I thought you were going to do the dishes two hours ago!" said Matt.

"Oh," I said, looking up from my phone.

This was a regular occurrence in our house during the beginning of our marriage. To him, it seemed like I simply didn't care, when what really happened was that I'd get distracted on my way to the kitchen and start doing something else. I understand now how frustrating it must've been for him to have a partner he couldn't rely on. My distractibility and disorganization meant my husband had to stretch himself thin to keep things in order.

Attention-related problems and forgetfulness mean the ADHDer's partner keeps losing essential items, forgetting important dates, and failing to follow through on commitments. Over time, this can make the neurotypical partner feel exhausted, unheard, and uncared for, giving rise to resentment.

Money Matters

People with ADHD are more likely than non-ADHDers to struggle with finances. The need for immediate rewards causes us to overlook long-term consequences of our decisions, leading to impulsive purchases. This leads to money problems that negatively impact our relationship with our significant other. Numerous studies link financial distress with lower relationship satisfaction.[51]

Our yearning for novelty and excitement means we're always on the move, frequently changing jobs, and adopting new hobbies and interests. This can have a negative impact on our finances. Switching jobs and investing in new hobbies may frequently burn through our savings and shift the financial burden to the neurotypical partner.

The ADHD tendency to be reckless with money can place a couple in a precarious financial situation, cause undue stress on the neurotypical partner, and cause the quality of the relationship to deteriorate.

Rejection Sensitivity

As people with ADHD, we don't handle criticism well. Being called out for not fulfilling our responsibilities or because we forget to do as we promised may trigger a disproportionate response from us. We may become so overwhelmed by intense emotions when our partners try to address a specific issue that we shut down the conversation or fly off the handle.

Even when our partners simply voice concern, our ADHD brains may perceive those statements as demeaning or patronizing. This places us in a defensive position, affecting our ability to commit to bringing about meaningful change. Our perceived sense of rejection also causes us to read too much into mundane interactions and to dissect and overanalyze minute details, leading to misunderstandings.

Parenting With ADHD

Parenting is hard enough. Add ADHD to the mix, and you have the recipe for unending chaos. Don't get me wrong; I don't regret or resent being a mother. Taking care of three kids is draining sometimes, but the countless moments of unadulterated joy make it all worth it. Moreover, as previously mentioned, it wasn't until I became a mother that I became aware of my ADHD symptoms. Each day presented new challenges, making me confront my weaknesses and overcome my limitations. Motherhood changed me for the better, but it wasn't an easy journey. My ADHD made the demands of being a parent twice as hard.

Parenting challenges multiply twofold when ADHD is part of the picture. Inattention, emotional dysregulation, and impulsivity impact our ability to fulfill our responsibilities as caregivers. Here are some ways ADHD influences our parenting:

- **Helping children weather emotional storms.** Emotional dysregulation makes it difficult to deal with the little ones' tantrums. Children look to their parents to help guide them through intense emotions. ADHD makes it difficult to manage big feelings and model calm for our kids.
- **Building a strong parent-child bond.** As adult women with ADHD juggling multiple tasks at once, we're more likely to dissociate from the chaos by using our phones. This affects our ability to spend quality time with our kids and foster deep connections.
- **Planning ahead and strategizing.** Taking care of the little ones requires a lot of planning, troubleshooting, and problem solving —tasks that demand strong executive functioning skills. Parents need

to plan and organize to get things done, alter and adjust their plans based on their children's needs, and respond to emergencies. All this can become too overwhelming for the ADHD parent, and we may find ourselves struggling to keep up with daily demands and responsibilities.

- **Organizing and managing.** Adults with ADHD have a hard time maintaining organized spaces, following a consistent daily schedule, and managing time effectively. As parents, we're not only responsible for keeping ourselves organized, but there's the added pressure of managing our children's lives as well. Time blindness and disorganization make it difficult to fulfill this responsibility. Failing to attend to our children's needs generates feelings of shame and self-resentment, which only serve to worsen the ADHD symptoms.

ADHD may hamper our ability to form deep, enriching friendships, long-lasting relationships, and meaningful connections with our children. Still, there's a lot we can do to overcome the challenges we face. The following discussion explores ways to enhance our relationships and foster stronger connections with our loved ones.

Finding Your Tribe: Navigating Relationship Problems

A few months into my relationship with Matt, we seemed headed for disaster. I'd prepared myself for another breakup when Matt surprised me by suggesting couples counseling instead. Over the next three months, we learned to understand each other better and communicate more effectively. The sessions not only saved our relationship but also strengthened our connection.

My short-lived relationships and friendships taught me not to rely on others. So, when Matt proposed, I thought he'd made a mistake, and I kept waiting for him to change his mind. Even after exchanging vows at the altar and becoming a mom to three beautiful children, I kept expecting him to leave. It wasn't until I was diagnosed with ADHD that I realized my RSD was to blame for my negative thinking. Coming to terms with my own shortcomings and devising strategies for working my way around common ADHD pitfalls allowed me to strengthen my bond with my spouse.

Open and honest communication is crucial in a relationship between an ADHDer and a non-ADHD individual. Here are some strategies for overcoming relationship problems and making your partner feel cared for.

How to Communicate Better with Your Partner

Communication with an ADHD partner can be challenging. The neurotypical person in the relationship often feels unheard, while the ADHD-partner feels attacked. Instead of trying to see things from each other's perspectives during an argument, both partners get themselves emotionally wound up and walk away feeling hurt and wronged. The entire episode achieves nothing but adds more stress and drama to the situation. Here are some tips to establish better communication with your partner so that, instead of locking horns, the two of you work together to find solutions.

1. **Pause and breathe.** People with ADHD are quick to react. It's tempting to say the first thing that pops into our minds when we're feeling overwhelmed. We may detect an accusatory undertone in the first few words chosen by our partners, and we flip out. It's important that partners approach challenging conversations when they're both feeling calm. If possible, schedule difficult conversations at a time and place that will be free from interruptions or disturbances. Remember to pause and breathe before responding or making a statement.
2. **Focus on your feelings.** Use more "I" statements than "you" statements. For instance, say, "I feel that you don't listen to me" rather than "You never listen to me!" This shows your partner your perspective without making them feel attacked. It also highlights the impact your partner's actions have on you, which builds empathy. Importantly, it helps clear misunderstandings by allowing your partner to explain their side of the story. It's highly likely that it wasn't their intention to hurt; they were simply thoughtless with their actions or words.

3. **Assume the best.** People with ADHD tend to have negativity bias, courtesy of RSD. Knowing this, unless your partner explicitly states the worst, don't automatically assume that to be the case. It's always best to assume positive intent. For instance, if your partner asks you whether you dropped the kids off at school on time, avoid perceiving the question as a personal attack. Take the question for what it is. Don't try to find hidden meaning in it. Put the brakes on your overthinking mind, and if that doesn't help, ask your partner about it directly instead of jumping to conclusions.
4. **Focus on the positives.** For a woman with ADHD, it's easy to fall into the habit of criticizing your partner or always seeing the worst in them. This constant blame game can destroy the relationship over time. While it's important to discuss problems and work together to find solutions, it's equally important to encourage, validate, and appreciate each other. So don't withhold praise when it's due. Compliment your partner for making the effort to change. The next time your partner does something kind or thoughtful, no matter how small, make it a point to let them know how it made you feel. This helps the other person feel seen and encourages them to repeat that behavior.
5. **Avoid shutting down.** People with ADHD tend to dissociate when things feel too overwhelming or the stakes seem too high. We may space out in the middle of conversations or begin scrolling on our phones to detach from the present situation. It's vital for our neurotypical partners to understand what's going on and not get the impression that we simply don't care. It's perfectly okay, when we feel overwhelmed, to take a break and pick things up where we left off after we've had some time to ourselves. Taking a five-minute break, moving to somewhere quiet, and practicing mindfulness meditation will not only help de-escalate the situation but also place us in a better state of mind to approach the problem.

Good communication is the bedrock of strong relationships. Sadly, ADHD can make simple and straightforward conversations feel intense and overwhelming. By applying the tips listed above, we can practice sharing our views respectfully while allowing our partners space to voice their concerns.

How to Make Friendships Last

Not having a strong support system can take a toll on our mental and emotional health. However, ADHD makes maintaining the friendship equation tricky. With a healthy dose of self-awareness and a few small changes, we can learn to nurture and strengthen our friendships and make them last a lifetime. Here are a few tips we should keep in mind to sustain friendships.

1. **Build self-awareness.** Do you feel distant from your friends? The first step you can take to save a friendship is to build self-awareness. Pay attention to your behavior. Do you actively listen when you're with your friend? Do you interrupt often? Is your friend the one who always makes plans to meet up or stay connected? If so, commit to taking small steps each day to change your behavior. Focus on becoming a good listener, check up on your friend by sending a text, or make plans to meet and catch up. Small things can make a huge difference.
2. **Nurture your friendships.** Friendships need generous doses of TLC. Keep track of birthdays or other important dates on your phone's calendar app and set reminders. Let your friends know you've been thinking about them. The next time you meet, mention something they said the last time you got together and how you kept thinking about it. Plan activities you love to do with your friend, and follow through with them. Pick a gift for them while traveling. Make sure you're there for them in their time of need. Create a safe space for them to share their thoughts and emotions with you without fear of judgment.
3. **Avoid overcommitting.** Nothing else destroys trust between two people more effectively than one of those two consistently failing to deliver on their promises. Avoid agreeing to plans or making commitments to help on the spur of the moment. Ask for some time to think about the suggestion and check your schedule. Be honest with yourself. Will you have enough time to help your friend with everything else that's on your plate? Avoid unrealistic optimism. It's better to be open and honest with them about why you can't commit to something rather than getting their hopes up and

letting them down later. When you do agree to a plan, make it a priority and follow through.

It's common for women with ADHD to feel ostracized because of their symptoms. A strong support system helps us combat loneliness. Friends lift us up when we're feeling down, helping us bounce back from setbacks and work toward achieving our goals. With a few simple tweaks, we can make sure our loved ones feel cherished and important.

How to Be a Better Parent

Relationships can be tough to maintain, but parenting is an entirely different ball game. In addition to being a great listener and an attentive caregiver, a parent must also be a fantastic organizer, a calm referee, and an incredible manager. It's a tall order for any adult, especially one with a faulty working memory and executive dysfunction, but, as with every other ADHD behavior, parenting style can be changed. Here are some ways to do that:

1. **Follow a consistent daily routine.** The more structured and predictable your day, the fewer meltdowns and chaos you'll experience. Create a daily routine using the template provided in Chapter 3.
2. **Create a daily checklist.** Start the day with a daily checklist to make sure you attend to important tasks. If your children are old enough, get them to create checklists for themselves. Offer rewards when your kids complete all the tasks on their lists to keep them motivated.
3. **Keep a go bag ready.** Avoid last-minute scrambles by keeping your go bags at the ready. For school kids, prepare their school bags at night and hang them on a peg near the door. For babies and younger children, stuff a bag with essential items for when you need to leave in a rush: toys, snacks, formula, burp cloths, and a board book.
4. **Everything in its place.** Designate specific areas in your home for specific items and activities. For example, keep the learning supplies and stationery in one area, toys and video games in another; keep hair accessories in a container in one drawer; reserve an area for

arts and crafts activities, and keep the supplies nearby. Designated areas eliminate the need for guesswork and minimize overwhelm while keeping the house organized.

5. **Set reminders.** Visual reminders are your best friend. If there's something that needs to be done, write it down on a colorful sticky note and stick it on the fridge or any other area where it'll be noticeable. Set reminders on your phones for important appointments, school events, and birthday parties.
6. **Schedule quality time with your kids.** It's easy to get so caught up in the daily struggle of managing and organizing multiple tasks that you neglect spending quality time with your kids. Children yearn for connection with their parents, and it's essential for you to make them feel heard and seen. Schedule an activity with your kids—something as simple as sitting down with them to color, gardening, or cooking together. Make sure you're fully present during this time and allow yourself to enjoy their company.

ADHD makes navigating the ups and downs of relationships all the more challenging. People with ADHD tend to wear their hearts on their sleeves. While our symptoms place us at a slight disadvantage, it's important to acknowledge all the good things our neurospicy brains have to offer. We may be emotional at times, but we're honest about how we feel. Our spontaneity and energy keep the spark alive in romantic relationships. We're full of unique and creative ideas and possess unquenchable curiosity and zest for life. Despite our symptoms, we have a lot of love, kindness, and compassion to offer.

Up ahead in chapter 7, we'll dive into our wallets as we learn how to manage our finances and budget effectively.

Exercise 6

The Communication Tune-Up

Good communication is the linchpin of strong relationships. By pausing to notice and reflect on our speaking habits, we can improve our communication skills. This exercise is designed to help you become more aware of your communication style and make changes where necessary to achieve deep and meaningful interactions with others.

Step 1: Do a quick communication self-check. In the list below, check the statements that apply to you.

- ☐ I interrupt people often.
- ☐ I often lose my train of thought or forget what I was about to say mid-sentence.
- ☐ I tend to overshare.
- ☐ I have a hard time listening to others.
- ☐ I often forget what people tell me.
- ☐ I catch myself zoning out during long conversations.
- ☐ I accidentally say things that come off as blunt, rude, or too honest.
- ☐ I replay conversations in my head, wondering if I said the wrong thing.
- ☐ I react harshly to criticism.
- ☐ I tend to take things personally and get upset during conversations.
- ☐ I spend hours overanalyzing what others said.

Step 2: Reflect on a recent conversation. Think about a recent interaction that didn't go as you had planned. Maybe you ended up giving the wrong impression or failed to express yourself well. Take a few minutes to think about that conversation, your choice of words, and how it made you feel afterward.

   a. Who were you talking with? What's type of your relationship do you have with that person? How did the conversation unfold?

   _____
   _____
   _____
   _____
   _____
   _____
   _____

   b. How did you feel when the conversation started veering off track? How did you feel after the conversation ended?

   _____
   _____
   _____
   _____

_____

_____

_____

   c. What do you think you could've done differently?

_____

_____

_____

_____

_____

_____

_____

Step 3: Build your communication toolbox. Let's build a toolbox of skills you can use the next time you're conversing with someone. In the list below, check the communication skills you want to try out. Practice them for a week. Once you've mastered a particular skill, move on to the next one.

- ☐ Pause before you respond.
- ☐ Listen patiently and try not to interrupt.
- ☐ Try to see things from others' perspectives.
- ☐ See the bigger picture and don't take everything as a personal affront.
- ☐ Ask yourself, after the conversation, whether there is some way you could have improved your part in it.
- ☐ Ask for clarification before making an assumption.

☐ Repeat what you heard.
☐ Write important things down.
☐ Take breaks mid-conversation if emotions run high.

Step 4: Re-do the conversation that didn't go well.

Imagine you could re-do the conversation you wrote about in Step 2 above. Consider how you would approach it now, using one or more of the skills in your toolbox under Step 3 above.

1. What would you say differently or not say at all? How would you act differently?

---

2. Which communication skill that you checked in Step 3 above do you think you need to work on the most? Why?

20-Minute Challenges

"To effectively communicate, we must realize that we are all different in the way we perceive the world and use this understanding as a guide to our communication with others."

— Tony Robbins

- **Pause and reflect.** The next time you find yourself fuming over something a person has said, pause and take a deep breath. Grab a pen and paper and divide the paper into two columns. In the left column, write down your assumptions about the person or the situation (for example, "My partner keeps finding fault in everything I do."). In the right column, write down the words your partner used, and ask yourself what they were trying to communicate (perhaps, "I keep forgetting to pay the bills, and my partner wants me to know they're frustrated by it.").
- **Review your daily schedule.** Take a look at your daily schedule. Do you put aside some time daily for self-care? If not, incorporate a thirty-minute walk or exercise session into your routine. Squeeze in a few minutes for your nighttime skin care, and see if you can add some morning yoga. Taking better care of yourself will make you more capable of taking care of others. So make sure your cup is full.
- **Call a friend.** Is there a friend you haven't spoken to or met with

in a long time? Send them a message and schedule a date. Follow through with your plan and meet up with them.

Chapter 7
Surviving Financial Thunderstorms
Budgeting and Getting Your Finances In Order

"Rule No. 1: Never lose money. Rule No. 2: Never forget Rule No. 1."

— *Warren Buffett*

Nothing used to stress me out quite as much as sitting down to pay the bills and budget for monthly expenses. I could never get around to budgeting and managing finances. The moment I'd get my paycheck, I'd feel the itch to spend it. And spend, I did. Online shopping became the bane of my existence. Every minor inconvenience or emotional upheaval felt like a sign from above for me to go online and click "Add to cart."

Managing finances is a Herculean task for ADHDers dealing with inattentiveness, impulsivity, and executive dysfunction. These symptoms significantly affect a person's ability to budget, track expenses, and save. A lack of sufficient dopamine reserves in the brain increases the likelihood of developing impulsive spending habits and makes it more challenging to adhere to a sound financial plan.

Read on as we investigate the role ADHD plays in money management, explore practical tips and strategies for curbing our spending, and get a better handle on our finances.

Common Financial Challenges

Managing finances relies on cognitive skills such as organization, planning, and impulse control. People with ADHD have a hard time summoning these cognitive abilities to keep their finances in check. Here's a brief overview of the challenges we face when it comes to managing our expenses and saving up:

- **Impulsivity.** We ADHDers frequently act on impulse and make spontaneous purchases, which makes it difficult to stick to a budget. Our need for immediate satisfaction makes it hard for us to resist buying the dress in the store window or a new pair of shoes, even when we don't need them.
- **Inattention.** For a long time, I struggled to pay bills on time and incurred late fees and overdraft charges. An ADHDer's attention deficits make it difficult to be mindful of expenses and manage savings wisely.
- **Executive function deficits.** Budgeting requires anticipating future expenses, planning, and prioritizing. ADHD can make these tasks rather daunting. We may delay carrying out these important but unpleasant tasks, which leads to more financial disorganization and stress later on.
- **Staying productive and focused at work.** People with ADHD are more likely than others to experience burnout at work. We frequently struggle with motivational slumps that cause our productivity to take a nosedive and put our jobs and careers in jeopardy. Additionally, we're prone to losing interest in our work and switching jobs frequently. All this has adverse effects on our finances.

The obstacles we face due to our ADHD make dealing with finances stressful and create poor financial habits. We may find the pressure of sorting through bills, managing money, pulling back on expenses, and making sound financial decisions overwhelming, and we may do our best to avoid these tasks. A lesson I learned after one too many financial mishaps is that it's better to address financial problems early on than wait for them to become more fearsome.

ADHD-Friendly Budgeting Techniques

Our ADHD brains trick us into thinking a problem will go away if we just look the other way. In reality, avoiding the problem only allows it to grow until it becomes completely unmanageable. One of the biggest reasons I used to avoid looking at my finances was that I knew managing them properly meant making hard decisions and sacrificing short-term rewards. I felt much better and more comfortable living inside my little bubble, splurging on shoes and handbags until my credit card was maxed out.

Like many adults with ADHD, I avoided directing my attention to my finances and hoped things would simply work out. While the bills and bank statements piled up, I busied myself with other tasks. What I didn't realize was that monitoring our cash flow is the only way to gain control of our money. And it's not as hard as we think it is! Now let's learn some ADHD-friendly budgeting techniques for staying on top of our finances.

Getting Started

The word *budget* evokes images of rigid rules and scarcity. Actually, it's anything but that. Budgeting, quite simply, is estimating and allocating our monthly earnings and expenditures. Essentially, budgeting means keeping an eye on the money flowing in and out and making small adjustments to retain more of it. Before you sit down to make your budget, you must have the following information on hand:

- your monthly take-home income
- your monthly essential expenses, including rent, groceries, mortgages and other loans, utilities, etc.
- the amount left over after subtracting your monthly expenses from your monthly income
- the due dates for bills and other payments

The first step to setting up your budget is to list your income and expenses. This will identify your spendings and savings. Start by listing all your sources of income, including your paychecks and side hustles, and sum them to determine your monthly earnings. Then make a list of all your expenses, including monthly bills, gas, groceries, rent, and discretionary spending. Subtract your expenses from your income to see what's left. If the result is a positive number, you can add it to your savings. If it's a negative number, you need to look for ways to cut your spending.

Creating a budget and establishing a spending allowance will make it easier for you to realize when you're going off the rails and enable you to resist the lure of the latest iPhone® or a new bottle of perfume. You learn to treat such purchases as luxuries, not must-haves.

Creating Separate Categories

As people with ADHD, we like to pile things up. Keeping all our money in one jumbled heap in a bank account may feel natural to us, but that makes it easy for us to overspend and overstretch our budgets. That's why it's important to sort our expenses by category.

The envelope method of categorizing monthly expenses works great for people with ADHD because it creates a clear picture in our minds. It is a simple cash system that involves placing an allotted amount of money inside an envelope for each budget category, such as gas, electricity, phone, and water. This ensures that all your essential monthly expenses are taken care of before you spend money on entertainment or luxuries. It's a method that works like a charm for many people with ADHD, but if handling cash is not your thing, try using a budgeting site like Empower Personal Dashboard™ or YNAB® to sort your money virtually. You can also use apps such as Emma™, Plum®, and Snoop® to track your expenses and categorize your budget.

Set Long-Term and Short-Term Goals

Financial goals help us stick to our budgets. If you create both short-term and long-term goals, it will help you stay on track with your expenses. For example, saving up for a vacation or a big purchase like a car may be your long-term goal. Meanwhile, saving a certain amount each month, building an emergency fund, and cutting back on an extra expense may be your short-term goals. Having a clear destination in mind helps us stay focused and motivated, making it easier for us to resist impulses and make tough decisions.

Tips on How to Save

Financial stability hinges on a robust savings plan. Building your savings keeps you focused on your financial goals, which is particularly beneficial for people with ADHD, who often struggle to control their impulsive spending. An effective saving strategy helps create a financial cushion, easing psychological burden, stress, and anxiety. Here are the steps you need to take to establish an effective savings strategy:

- **Identify your goals.** Specify what you're saving for—an emergency fund, a large purchase, retirement, or a vacation. Defined goals provide direction and fill us with the motivation required to pursue them.
- **Set realistic targets.** Create a roadmap for reaching your savings goals by breaking them down into smaller, more achievable targets. Divide the amount you plan to save in a year into a small amount you can easily put aside each month.
- **Make saving a priority.** Treat saving as a non-negotiable expense. Allocate a certain amount to your savings before indulging in luxuries or entertainment.
- **Save via direct deposit.** Skip decision-making: Automate the savings process by using direct deposit. Schedule an automatic monthly transfer from your checking account to your savings account, ensuring that a portion of your income is allocated to savings before you have the chance to spend it.
- **Explore savings apps.** Look into savings apps such as Moneybox® or Chip® to help you automate your savings by analyzing your purchases or setting aside a small amount regularly.

Strategies for Paying Off Debt

People with ADHD are highly likely to accumulate mountains of debt. Because we consistently prioritize short-term rewards, we are prone to overspending and getting sucked into the debt trap: borrowing money to pay off existing debt, only to end up increasing the amount we owe. A structured plan to do away with debt not only improves financial well-being but also alleviates stress and restores confidence in our abilities. Here are two debt payment methods that work well for people with ADHD:

- **Snowball method.** Start by paying off your smallest debts first. Keep making minimum payments on larger debts. Paying off small debts provides quick wins and keeps the motivation going for tackling the bigger debts.
- **Avalanche method.** Focus on the debts with the highest interest rates, and pay them off first to reduce the total interest paid over time.

Break the habit of using credit cards and piling on new debt. If your financial situation seems beyond repair, consider seeking professional help. Financial advisors or credit counselors can help you create a personalized plan to repay debt and sort out your finances.

Building Good Financial Habits

Ultimately, the best way to prevent accumulating debt is to develop good financial habits. That's easier said than done when you're grappling with ADHD. The best way forward is to take small steps, change small habits, and gradually work your way toward financial stability.

When I decided to get my finances in order, the first thing I did was become mindful of my spending habits. This meant holding on to every receipt and online purchase confirmation and keeping records of my expenses for a month. That gave me a good idea of where I spent most of my money. Using the information I'd gathered, I went about assessing the impact of different expenditures on my finances. Once I was honest with myself about my essential and non-essential purchases, I made adjustments to maximize my savings and crawl out of debt.

My efforts eventually paid off. Being more responsible with my money helped ease tensions in my marriage as well. I learned that developing good financial habits is the key to ending financial woes once and for all. Here are some money management tips and habits that you should consider adopting:

- **Clear goals.** Set clear savings goals, automate the savings process, and implement debt management strategies.
- **Set reminders.** Relying on our working memory is risky, so set reminders to pay bills, make debt repayments, and review your weekly or monthly spending.
- **Track expenses consistently.** Hold on to those receipts and record every purchase you make by entering it into your money management app or spreadsheet. This helps create an accurate idea of your spending habits.
- **Opt for cash.** Avoid using your credit or debit cards. Carrying only cash while shopping puts a tangible limit on your spending.
- **Wait it out.** Beat impulsive buying by creating a waiting period for non-essential purchases. Keep the duration long for pricier items. Waiting anywhere between twenty-four hours to a week can make the impulse fade and allow better sense to prevail.
- **Make shopping lists.** Create a shopping list before heading out to buy something. Strictly adhere to the list in hand and avoid buying non-essential items.

Money management is not an elusive skill that only neurotypical people can master. With a little practice, neurospicy folks, like you and me, can achieve greater financial stability by turning good financial practices into lifelong habits.

In the next chapter, we'll be turning our attention to our plates and analyzing what we eat. We'll also explore holistic practices and natural remedies to manage our symptoms, so please keep reading.

Exercise 7

The Weekly Financial Check-In

Use the template below to keep an eye on your income, expenses, and savings. Calculate the amount earned, saved, or spent at the end of each month to assess your financial situation.

Income Sources	Projected Amount	Week 1	Week 2	Week 3	Week 4	Monthly Total

Mikaela Salazar

Expenses	Projected Amount	Week 1	Week 2	Week 3	Week 4	Monthly Total

Savings (Long-term)	Projected Amount	Week 1	Week 2	Week 3	Week 4	Monthly Total

Savings (Short-term)	Projected Amount	Week 1	Week 2	Week 3	Week 4	Monthly Total

20-Minute Challenges

"Budgeting is telling your money where to go, instead of wondering where it went."

— John Barnes

- **Make a shopping list.** Make a list of items that you need to buy before heading to the grocery store or shopping mall. Review your budget and make sure these items are essential purchases. Challenge yourself to stick to your list while you shop.
- **Calculate your expenses.** Gather all the receipts, bills, and online purchases, and calculate your monthly expenses.
- **Ditch the credit card.** Challenge yourself to shop using only cash for a week. Take your credit and debit cards out of your wallet and avoid carrying them with you when you leave the house.

Chapter 8
What's Your Diet Got to Do With It?
Exploring Natural Remedies and Holistic Practices

"Let food be your medicine and medicine be your food."

— *Hippocrates*

My relationship with food has been a complicated one. Due to social pressure to look good and my periods of intense hyperfocus, I sometimes go for hours without eating. Then there are times when the stress of a work project or a messy house makes me want to binge on a bucket of fried chicken and a tub of ice cream.

I'd always struggled to maintain a consistent weight, but it was only after I did a deep dive into ADHD that I learned about the role my dopamine-deprived brain played in it. Women with ADHD are more vulnerable to developing eating disorders. A 2015 research report published in *CNS Spectrums*, the journal of the Neuroscience Education Institute, emphasized the close relation between ADHD, binge-eating disorder (BED), and obesity.[52] These conditions are likely to occur together due to shared neural pathways. That is, the parts of the brain affected by ADHD are the same regions that show dysfunction in patients suffering from obesity or BED. As a result, more than 30 percent of people with ADHD show disordered eating patterns.[53]

While executive dysfunction and emotional dysregulation make it difficult to resist unhealthy, decadent foods, an unbalanced diet leads to nutrient deficiencies and worsening ADHD symptoms. Let's investigate the link between ADHD and nutrition and how your food choices may be impacting your brain.

The Hidden Link Between ADHD And Nutrition

Women with ADHD face a significantly higher risk than other women of developing nutritional deficiencies. Our symptoms make it difficult for us to consistently eat a well-balanced, healthy diet. This makes us miss out on key nutrients such as omega-3 fatty acids, B vitamins, magnesium, zinc, and iron, which are all essential for proper brain functioning. Decreased levels of these micronutrients increases inattention, emotional problems, and hyperactivity.

In addition to providing an uninterrupted stream of much-needed nutrients, a healthy diet helps us maintain a consistent blood sugar level, which is necessary for regulating mood, focus, and energy. Forgetting to eat while we hyperfocus on a task can cause blood sugar to plunge, increasing agitation, brain fog, restlessness, poor focus, and fatigue. Meanwhile, snacking on carbohydrate-rich, sugary foods can cause blood sugar to spike, then crash soon afterward, worsening ADHD symptoms.

Women with ADHD are predisposed to eating disorders, which sabotage good nutrition. For instance, a study led by researchers at the Massachusetts General Hospital in Boston, MA, US, found girls with ADHD more prone to developing eating disorders, such as bulimia, BED, and anorexia, than their neurotypical counterparts.[54] Another study conducted in Perth, Western Australia, discovered that women with ADHD were more likely to develop iron deficiencies characterized by symptoms such as heavy menstrual bleeding, brain fog, anxiety, dizziness, fatigue, headaches, depression, and restless leg syndrome.[55]

These studies and others like them underscore the importance of good nutrition in women with ADHD, so let's take a closer look at some of the nutrients in question and the roles they play.

Iron

In addition to transporting oxygen to our muscles and organs, iron affects the production of dopamine. People with ADHD already have low reserves of dopamine, and iron deficiency further disrupts the production of this vital neurotransmitter. You can increase your iron intake by taking supplements or adding more iron-rich foods to your diet. Natural food sources of this magic mineral include meat, poultry, fish, whole grains, eggs, potatoes, peas, bananas, and legumes. You can increase the absorption of iron from these foods by increasing your intake of vitamin C, found in citrus fruits such as oranges and grapefruit.

Zinc

Our bodies need zinc for the production of several neurotransmitters, including GABA and dopamine. GABA is an inhibitory neurotransmitter that helps induce a state of calm by lowering stress, anxiety, and fear. Dairy, meat, poultry, eggs, whole grains, beans, nuts, and oysters are some natural sources for this essential chemical messenger.

Magnesium

If you find yourself tossing and turning during the night, a deficiency in magnesium could be the reason for your lack of sleep. Found in leafy greens, nuts, beans, legumes, and whole grains, this essential mineral maintains healthy sleep patterns. It influences the production of neurotransmitters that help us wind down and relax, thereby reducing anxiety and decreasing the body's stress response.

Omega-3 Fatty Acids

Found in fatty fish like salmon and tuna, omega-3 fatty acids play a key role in maintaining brain health. Due to the many health benefits of omega-3s, the American Psychiatric Association recommends that men, women, and children eat fish at least two or more times a week.[58] For people with ADHD, the Association advises adding 1 gram of fish oil to their daily diets.

Vitamin B

A diet low in B vitamins, particularly vitamins B6 and B12, can lead to increased irritability and fatigue in adults with ADHD. Maintaining healthy levels of these vitamins can increase alertness while decreasing anxiety and mood swings. Foods like tuna, salmon, spinach, and bananas are good sources of B vitamins.

Adaptogens

Adaptogens are plant substances found in roots, herbs, and mushrooms that help minimize stress and restore calm after a stressful situation. They're available as herbal supplements in the form of capsules or powders that can be added to drinks or sprinkled on food.

Adaptogens, such as Rhodiola rosea and ashwagandha, have been studied for their positive effect on brain functioning and have been shown to boost levels of dopamine and increase alertness. A group of Swedish researchers studying the role of adaptogens found that these plant substances significantly decreased study participants' sensitivity to stressors, improving their overall ability to handle stress and reducing fatigue.[56]

Exploring the ADHD Diet

The preceding discussion of nutrients gives rise to the question, "What should an ADHDer's diet look like?" A 2022 review published in the journal *Nutrients* linked diets high in processed carbohydrates, high in sugars, and low in fiber with intensified ADHD symptoms.[59] In contrast, nutrient-dense diets packed with vitamins, minerals, and dietary fibers, including the Mediterranean and DASH (dietary approaches to stop hypertension) diets, may improve symptoms and boost overall mental and physical health.

Foods to Choose

Here is a list of the foods we should eat more of to improve concentration and prevent our ADHD minds from drifting:

- **Protein.** Eggs, beans, cheese, nuts, and meat are good sources of protein. Try to include them in your breakfast or munch on them as afternoon snacks. Consuming more protein may even make ADHD medication work longer.
- **Complex carbohydrates.** These carbs are found in fruits and vegetables such as oranges, tangerines, pears, grapefruits, kiwis, and apples. Consuming more complex carbohydrates in the evening may help us sleep better.
- **Omega-3 fatty acids.** Foods containing omega-3s are, quite literally, brain foods. Reach for tuna, salmon, other white fish, Brazil nuts, olive oil, and canola oil. Alternatively, you can take omega-3 fatty acid supplements.

Foods to Avoid

Now that we know the foods we should eat, we need to identify the ones we should steer clear of.

- **Sugars.** Diets high in sugar may exacerbate ADHD symptoms. Limit sugar intake to less than 10 percent of your daily diet. In a two-thousand-calorie diet, no more than two hundred calories—almost twelve teaspoons—should come from sugar.[58] Avoid sugary drinks like sodas or fruit juices, candies, cakes, cookies, and processed and packaged foods high in sugar.
- **Simple carbohydrates.** Unlike complex carbohydrates, simple carbohydrates break down quickly in our bodies, causing blood sugar spikes. Moreover, they tend to have low nutritional content. Cut back on products made from white flour, potatoes without their skins, and white rice.
- **Saturated fats.** While fats are important in helping our bodies absorb vitamins, saturated fats do more harm than good. How can you differentiate saturated fats from unsaturated "good" fats? Saturated fats, such as butter, usually remain solid at room temperature, while unsaturated fats, such as canola oil, do not. A diet rich in saturated fats raises the levels of cholesterol in the blood, and some evidence suggests it may even worsen ADHD symptoms.

Avoid highly processed foods and fried foods prepared in lots of oil, lard, or butter.

The Elimination Diet

Do you ever notice your ADHD symptoms flaring up all of a sudden? The reason may lie in what you eat. Most of the food items that trigger ADHD symptoms belong to one of the categories under the "Foods to Avoid" heading above. Following the elimination diet could help you identify which foods trigger or worsen your ADHD symptoms so you can avoid those foods.

For this diet, you simply pick a particular ingredient or food that you suspect may be making your symptoms worse. Let's say you recently started munching on a specific type of chocolate bar and noticed an increase in your hyperactivity or impulsivity. Avoid eating it for a week and see if there's a change in your behavior. Foods that may trigger ADHD symptoms include these:

- Artificial colors, particularly red and yellow
- Food additives, including monosodium glutamate (MSG), aspartame, sodium benzoate, and nitrites
- Sugar
- Caffeine

ADHD Meal Prepping

My ADHD used to make meal planning, cooking, and cleaning up the mess afterward feel like one big chore. For me, meal prepping was a real game-changer. Now, not only do I plan what I'll cook and eat during the coming week, but I also do most of the prepping in advance. This cuts down the cooking time for each recipe and keeps the mess minimal.

What I like to do is prepare things in bulk at the beginning of each week. This includes two to three protein sources, such as salmon, boiled eggs, chicken, and minced beef, as well as plant-based proteins like tofu or canned legumes. I also prepare weekly servings of quinoa, rice, pasta, roasted vegetables, chopped raw veggies, and fruits.

To make it easier to whip up meals during the week, I cook and freeze base dishes or whole meals. I chop veggies and meats and cook large batches of base recipes like meatballs, curries, marinades, pestos, and vinaigrettes. I transfer these to plastic food storage bags and toss them into the freezer to use later in preparing a variety of dishes. When I have the time, I freeze fully cooked meals, including stove-top lasagna, soup, pasta, casseroles, quiche, muffins, and banana bread, which are ready to eat once heated up.

Unraveling Genetic Anomalies

We've talked about the differences between ADHD and non-ADHD brains and how they set us apart from one another. One such difference lies in the mutation of the MTHFR gene. Although not everyone with ADHD has this mutation, research suggests a link between the MTHFR gene and ADHD, underscoring the impact of nutrition on brain function. So, what exactly is this gene, why does it matter, and how does good nutrition come into play for those who have the mutation?

MTHFR stands for (take a deep breath, and read it slowly) methy-lene-tetra-hydro-folate re-duc-tase. Phew! That's one big name! The MTHFR gene signals the body to produce the MTHFR enzyme. Think of an enzyme as a sort of energy drink that speeds up various processes in your body. One such process is the breakdown of vitamin B9, known as folate or folic acid. The MTHFR enzyme transforms folate into a methylfolate, a form that can be easily absorbed by our cells. Methylfolate, in turn, converts amino acids (the building blocks of proteins) into neurotransmitters such as dopamine. The process works like a smooth chain reaction.[57]

But a mutation in the MTHFR gene disrupts this process. Imagine a bunch of factory workers assembling a product on a conveyor belt. If there is a mechanical problem, the conveyor belt slows down, and the workers move less product down the line. A mutation in the MTHFR gene is similar to this mechanical problem: It disrupts the gene's function, and less dopamine is produced. This leads to impulse control problems. A person with this mutation may have large amounts of folate in their body but not enough methylfolate to produce adequate amounts of dopamine.

The MTHFR mutation can be confirmed through blood tests. If you have both ADHD and the mutation, it's important to manage both by taking folate and vitamin B supplements. Increasing the amount of folate-containing foods in your diet may also help. These include dark leafy greens like asparagus and spinach, eggs, beef liver, fortified cereals, and legumes.[57]

ADHD and Heart Rate Variability (HRV)

Turn your hand over, palm up, and place two fingers of your other hand on your upturned wrist. Do you feel the rhythmic flow of blood through your veins? Count the beats for sixty seconds, and you'll know your heart rate, which is the number of times your heart beats per minute.

Heart rate variability (HRV) is a measure of how frequently your heart's rate fluctuates between high and low. Higher HRV means the heart rate switches between high and low often, which indicates good heart health.[60] This is because higher HRV indicates a well-regulated nervous system capable of handling stress and changes in the environment. A low HRV indicates decreased ability to handle stress. In individuals with ADHD, low HRV can lead to increased sensitivity to stress, emotional dysregulation, impulsivity, and a lack of attention.

HRV also gives us an idea of our vagal tone.[60] This tone is the activity of the vagus nerve, which sends signals to the brain. Imagine a long highway running up your spinal cord, all the way from your gut to your brain. That's your vagus nerve, the interstate highway of your body. High HRV indicates good vagal tone. Imagine the traffic running smoothly along the highway without any interruptions. Low HRV, on the other hand, could mean trouble brewing along the vagus nerve.

When our body experiences long periods of infection, chronic stress, and inflammation, traffic along the vagus nerve becomes congested, disrupting the signals being transmitted along this important highway. Telltale signs that the vagal tone is not working as it should include fatigue, muscle aches, brain fog, and headaches.

Research shows that people with ADHD tend to have low HRV, which has a negative impact on overall health.[60] Low HRV can lead to a dysregulated nervous system and decreased vagal tone, which is associated with a number of health problems, such as an increased stress response, trouble self-regulating, hypertension, fatigue, and depression.

Tracking your HRV is a great way to keep a check on your health. You can use a heart rate monitor such as a Fitbit® or an Apple Watch®. If you notice a low HRV, try to increase it by using one of the treatments described below under the "Treating Low HRV" heading. After three months, take your HRV reading again to see if there's any difference. It takes time to raise HRV, and you may need to continue your treatment for a year before you notice significant improvement.

Treating Low HRV

HRV is an important indicator of our physical and mental well-being. While an occasional low reading of HRV isn't anything to worry about, consistently low HRV can be a cause for concern. Ways to treat low HRV include the following:

- **Deep breathing.** Regular deep breathing exercises calm the nervous system, improving attention and reducing anxiety.
- **Exposure to cold.** A cold shower or cold compresses can help stimulate the vagus nerve, activating the body's calm response (the parasympathetic pathway), which controls HRV.
- **Mindfulness meditation.** Another way to induce calm and raise HRV is mindfulness meditation. Mindfulness exercises, practiced even for one minute per day, can considerably improve our ability to deal with stressful situations and improve HRV.
- **Consistent sleep.** Getting eight hours of restful sleep every night not only reduces stress and anxiety but also increases HRV, boosting overall health.
- **Regular exercise.** Daily physical exercise helps strengthen our nervous systems and releases feel-good chemicals such as endorphins, which improve focus and self-control.
- **Diet.** Anti-inflammatory diets that include foods such as leafy greens, whole grains, and omega-3 fatty acids boost brain function while improving HRV.

- **Yoga and tai chi.** Both tai chi and yoga are shown to improve HRV by enhancing parasympathetic activity. For people with ADHD, these practices help reduce impulsivity, improve body awareness, and promote emotional regulation over time.

As women with ADHD, it's easy to lose ourselves in the daily scramble. Self-care and nutrition go to the back burner while we struggle to take care of everyone else's needs. It's important to take a step back from the hustle and bustle of everyday life and make ourselves the priority. Eating well, exercising, and getting adequate sleep are all acts of self-love that help us recharge and get back in the game.

Exercise 8

ADHD Weekly Meal Plan

1. Use the template below to create a weekly meal plan. Include the foods you should eat more often and try not to include the foods you should avoid. Make sure to include foods discussed in this chapter that contain essential nutrients.

Week of _____ (date)

	Breakfast	Lunch	Dinner	Snacks
Monday				
Tuesday				
Wednesday				
Thursday				
Friday				
Saturday				
Sunday				

2. Make a list of dishes you want to prep in advance.

a. _____
b. _____
c. _____
d. _____
e. _____
f. _____
g. _____

3. Write down your grocery list for the recipes for dishes listed in 2. above.

_____

_____

_____

_____

_____

_____

_____

_____

_____

_____

_____

_____

4. ADHD Elimination Diet

In the first column of the table below, list the food items you intend to eliminate from your diet for one week. In the ADHD Symptom Severity column, for each food listed, identify your symptoms, such as hyperactivity, impulsiveness, and emotional dysregulation, and for each symptom, also write down the severity level, using a scale of 1 to 10, from least to most severe. In the One Week Update column, rate each symptom again after one week to see if the severity has changed.

Food Item	ADHD Symptom Severity	One Week Update

20-Minute Challenges

> *"The food you eat can be either the safest and most powerful form of medicine or the slowest form of poison."*
>
> — *Ann Wigmore*

- **Kitchen sweep.** Set the timer for twenty minutes, and go through your pantry. Find three items that could be triggering your ADHD symptoms, and toss them out.
- **Consider taking supplements.** Get in touch with your doctor or other health care provider to look into taking supplements.
- **Nutrient-dense foods.** Find a new recipe online that contains high doses of nutrients that boost brain health, and try it out.

Final Thoughts
Replacing Doubt with Self-Compassion

There's nothing else quite as daunting as being confronted with a lifelong mental health condition at the age of forty. The revelation that I had ADHD was life-altering. It was like having a haze lifted from my mind. Things I couldn't understand before started to make sense. Why was I always late to work? Why couldn't I become more organized? Why was it so difficult for me to get off the couch and get on with household chores? Knowing that the struggles I faced were due to my brain chemistry made me capable of extending compassion to myself. After interacting with countless women with ADHD over the past five years, I've come to the sad conclusion that self-compassion is what most of us lack.

My purpose in writing this book is to give you an idea of how your ADHD mind works and what you can do about it. While being neurodivergent gives us numerous unique advantages, in some respects, it also makes life more challenging. We need to acknowledge both the downsides and the upsides of ADHD; doing so is the true form of self-compassion. Life with ADHD is neither a bed of roses nor as gloomy as some people would have you believe. Life with ADHD is just that, life—sometimes challenging, sometimes beautiful, and always worth it.

Despite the tough times my ADHD causes, I can't help but feel grateful for my unique, unbridled mind. Although frustrating at times, my ADHD brain consistently generates interesting and creative ideas that have helped me

Final Thoughts

stand out numerous times in my career. My ADHD also makes me more hopeful in the face of adversity than I would otherwise be. Unburdened by convention and quick to abandon reason, my ADHD brain has shown remarkable resilience during difficult times. The struggles I encounter due to my neurodivergent thinking also open my heart to being more empathetic and kinder to others. To me, all these attributes—kindness, empathy, creativity, courage, resilience—are nothing short of superpowers.

References

1. Martin, J. (2024). Why are females less likely to be diagnosed with ADHD in childhood than males? *The Lancet Psychiatry*. 11(4). 303 - 310. https://doi.org/10.1016/S2215-0366(24)00010-5
2. Hoogman, M., Bralten, J., Hibar, D. P., Mennes, M., Zwiers, M. P., Schweren, L. S. J., Van Hulzen, K. J. E., Medland, S. E., Shumskaya, E., Jahanshad, N., De Zeeuw, P., Szekely, E., Sudre, G., Wolfers, T., Onnink, A. M. H., Dammers, J. T., Mostert, J. C., Vives-Gilabert, Y., Kohls, G., . . . Franke, B. (2017). Subcortical brain volume differences in participants with attention deficit hyperactivity disorder in children and adults: a cross-sectional mega-analysis. *The Lancet Psychiatry*, 4(4), 310–319. https://doi.org/10.1016/s2215-0366(17)30049-4
3. Cronkleton, E. (2021, August 13). *What are the differences between an ADHD brain and a neurotypical brain*. https://www.medicalnewstoday.com/articles/adhd-brain-vs-normal-brain#structure
4. Goldstein, S. (n.d.). Intelligence and ADHD. *Sam Goldstein & Associates*. https://samgoldstein.com/resources/articles/general/intelligence-and-adhd.aspx
5. Roth, E. (2025, February 25). *What are the 3 types of ADHD?* Healthline. https://www.healthline.com/health/adhd/three-types-adhd#treatment
6. Low, K. (2023, December 6). *ADHD in Women: Signs and symptoms*. Verywell Mind. https://www.verywellmind.com/add-symptoms-in-women-20394
7. Cleveland Clinic. (n.d.). *ADHD medications: How they work & side effects*. Cleveland Clinic. https://my.clevelandclinic.org/health/treatments/11766-adhd-medication
8. Sedgwick, J.A., Merwood, A. & Asherson, P. The positive aspects of attention deficit hyperactivity disorder: a qualitative investigation of successful adults with ADHD. *ADHD Atten Def Hyp Disord* 11, 241–253 (2019). https://doi.org/10.1007/s12402-018-0277-6
9. Boot, N., Nevicka, B., & Baas, M. (2017). Creativity in ADHD: Goal-Directed Motivation and Domain Specificity. *Journal of Attention Disorders*, 24(13), 1857-1866. https://doi.org/10.1177/1087054717727352
10. Kollins, S. H., & Adcock, R. A. (2014). ADHD, altered dopamine neurotransmission, and disrupted reinforcement processes: implications for smoking and nicotine dependence. *Progress in neuro-psychopharmacology & biological psychiatry*, 52, 70–78. https://doi.org/10.1016/j.pnpbp.2014.02.002
11. Leo, D., Sukhanov, I., Zoratto, F., et al. (2018). Pronounced hyperactivity, cognitive dysfunctions, and BDNF dysregulation in dopamine transporter knock-out rats. *The Journal of Neuroscience*, 38(8), 1959–1972. https://doi.org/10.1523/jneurosci.1931-17.2018
12. Silva, S. (2024, October 10). *What is the role of dopamine in ADHD?* Healthline. https://www.healthline.com/health/adhd/adhd-dopamine#treatment

References

13. Hirsch, O., Chavanon, M. L., & Christiansen, H. (2019). Emotional dysregulation subgroups in patients with adult Attention-Deficit/Hyperactivity Disorder (ADHD): a cluster analytic approach. *Scientific Reports*, 9(1). https://doi.org/10.1038/s41598-019-42018-y

14. Talarovicová, A., Kršková, L., & Kiss, A. (2007). Some assessments of the amygdala role in suprahypothalamic neuroendocrine regulation: A minireview. *Endocrine Regulations*, 41(4), 155–162. https://pubmed.ncbi.nlm.nih.gov/18257652

15. Hulvershorn, L. A., Mennes, M., Castellanos, F. X., Di Martino, A., Milham, M. P., Hummer, T. A., & Roy, A. K. (2014). Abnormal amygdala functional connectivity associated with emotional lability in children with attention-deficit/hyperactivity disorder. *Journal of the American Academy of Child and Adolescent Psychiatry*, 53(3), 351–61.e1. https://doi.org/10.1016/j.jaac.2013.11

16. Centre, A. (2024, September 9). *Effective ways to fight against ADHD & overthinking*. The ADHD Centre. https://www.adhdcentre.co.uk/ways-to-fight-against-adhd-overthinking/

17. Rodriguez, R. (2023b, August 1). *What is ADHD Paralysis?* My Psychiatrist. https://mypsychiatrist.com/blog/what-is-adhd-paralysis/

18. Brain & Behavior Laboratory, Department of Psychology, Curry College, & Edward Justin Modestino. (2024). Rejection Sensitivity Dysphoria in Attention-Deficit/Hyperactivity Disorder: A Case series. In *Acta Scientific Neurology* [Case Series]. https://doi.org/10.31080/ASNE.2024.07.0762

19. Babinski, D. E., Kujawa, A., Kessel, E. M., Arfer, K. B., & Klein, D. N. (2018). Sensitivity to Peer Feedback in Young Adolescents with Symptoms of ADHD: Examination of Neurophysiological and Self-Report Measures. *Journal of Abnormal Child Psychology*, 47(4), 605–617. https://doi.org/10.1007/s10802-018-0470-2

20. Conway, S. (2023, October 18). *Meditation and the autonomic nervous system*. Mindworks Meditation & Buddhist Path. https://mindworks.org/blog/meditation-autonomic-nervous-system/

21. Murnan, A. (2025, February 14). *What is ADHD justice sensitivity?* https://www.medicalnewstoday.com/articles/adhd-justice-sensitivity#1

22. Brown, T. E., PhD. (2024, April 8). *The adult ADHD mind: Executive Function connections*. ADDitude. https://www.additudemag.com/inside-the-add-mind/?srsltid=AfmBOorKeuQkgQhBgjLwpGAIuZA3UBtjYx82ewiArZCzBT9jigiI8kow

23. Barkley, R., PhD. (2024, January 29). *What is executive function? 7 Deficits tied to ADHD*. ADDitude. https://www.additudemag.com/7-executive-function-deficits-linked-to-adhd/

24. Dana. (2024, December 6). *Executive Function Disorder & ADHD: Their Differences & How They Tie Together*. ADDA - Attention Deficit Disorder Association. https://add.org/executive-function-disorder/

25. Weissenberger, S., Schonova, K., Büttiker, P., Fazio, R., Vnukova, M., Stefano, G. B., & Ptacek, R. (2021). Time perception is a focal symptom of attention-deficit/hyperactivity disorder in adults. *Medical Science Monitor*, 27, e933766. https://doi.org/10.12659/MSM.933766

References

26. Brock, T. D. (2021). The study of microorganisms in situ: Progress and problems. *Advances in Microbial Physiology*, 78, 1-24. https://doi.org/10.1016/bs.ampbs.2021.01.001
27. Blum, K., Chen, A. L. C., Braverman, E. R., Comings, D. E., Chen, T. J. H., Arcuri, V., Blum, S. H., Downs, B. W., Waite, R. L., Notaro, A., Lubar, J., Williams, L., Prihoda, T. J., Palomo, T., & Oscar-Berman, M. (2008). Attention-deficit-hyperactivity disorder and reward deficiency syndrome. *Neuropsychiatric Disease and Treatment*, 893. https://doi.org/10.2147/ndt.s2627
28. Roselló, B., Berenguer, C., Baixauli, I., Mira, Á., Martinez-Raga, J., & Miranda, A. (2020b). Empirical examination of executive functioning, ADHD associated behaviors, and functional impairments in adults with persistent ADHD, remittent ADHD, and without ADHD. *BMC Psychiatry*, 20(1). https://doi.org/10.1186/s12888-020-02542-y
29. Mette, C. (2023). Time perception in adult ADHD: Findings from a decade—A review. *International Journal of Environmental Research and Public Health*, 20(4), 3098. https://doi.org/10.3390/ijerph20043098
30. Farley, J., Risko, E. F., & Kingstone, A. (2013). Everyday attention and lecture retention: the effects of time, fidgeting, and mind wandering. *Frontiers in Psychology*, 4. https://doi.org/10.3389/fpsyg.2013.00619
31. Birdee, G., Nelson, K., Wallston, K., Nian, H., Diedrich, A., Paranjape, S., Abraham, R., & Gamboa, A. (2023). Slow breathing for reducing stress: The effect of extending exhale. *Complementary Therapies in Medicine*, 73, 102937. https://doi.org/10.1016/j.ctim.2023.102937
32. Henderson, E. (2021, May 14). *Yoga and breathing exercises have a positive effect on children with ADHD*. News-Medical. https://www.news-medical.net/news/20210514/Yoga-and-breathing-exercises-have-a-positive-effect-on-children-with-ADHD.aspx
33. Eißfeller, S. (2023, January 9). *The perfect sleep routine for ADHD brains: 10-3-2-1-0*. Inflow. https://www.getinflow.io/post/sleep-better-with-adhd-the-10321o-routine
34. Sleep Foundation. (n.d.). *ADHD and sleep problems: How are they related?* https://www.sleepfoundation.org/mental-health/adhd-and-sleep
35. Johns Hopkins Medicine. (n.d.). *The science of sleep: Understanding what happens when you sleep*. https://www.hopkinsmedicine.org/health/wellness-and-prevention/the-science-of-sleep-understanding-what-happens-when-you-sleep
36. Lunsford-Avery, J. R., & Kollins, S. H. (2018). Editorial Perspective: Delayed circadian rhythm phase: a cause of late-onset attention-deficit/hyperactivity disorder among adolescents?. *Journal of child psychology and psychiatry, and allied disciplines*, 59(12), 1248–1251. https://doi.org/10.1111/jcpp.12956
37. Sciberras E, Mulraney M, Mensah F, Oberklaid F, Efron D, Hiscock H. Sustained impact of a sleep intervention and moderators of treatment outcome for children with ADHD: a randomised controlled trial. *Psychological Medicine*. 2020;50(2):210-219. doi:10.1017/S0033291718004063

References

38. AARP. (n.d.). *Why missing sleep is worse for women than men.* https://www.aarp.org/health/healthy-living/info-2023/why-sleep-matters-more-for-women.html
39. Zuraikat, F. M., Aggarwal, B., Jelic, S. St-Onge, M.-P., & Laferrère, B. (2024). Chronic insufficient sleep in women impairs insulin sensitivity independent of adiposity changes: Results of a randomized trial. *Diabetes Care, 47*(1), 117–125. https://doi.org/10.2337/dc23-1145 Diabetes Journals+3
40. Makarem, N., Zuraikat, F. M., Scaccia, S. E., RoyChoudhury, A., & St-Onge, M.-P. (2021). Sustained mild sleep restriction increases blood pressure in women: An update from the American Heart Association Go Red for Women Strategically Focused Research Network. *Hypertension, 77*(5), e50–e52. https://doi.org/10.1161/HYPERTENSIONAHA.120.16370
41. Davis, S. (2023, June 28). *Obesity: Symptoms, causes, treatment.* WebMD. https://www.webmd.com/obesity/what-obesity-is
42. The ADHD Centre. (n.d.). *ADHD brain fog: Symptoms & prevention strategies.* https://www.adhdcentre.co.uk/adhd-brain-fog/
43. Surman, C. B. H., Adamson, J. J., Petty, C., Biederman, J., Kenealy, D. C., Levine, M., Mick, E., & Faraone, S. V. (2009). Association between attention-deficit/hyperactivity disorder and sleep impairment in adulthood: Evidence from a large controlled study. *The Journal of Clinical Psychiatry, 70*(11), 1523–1529. https://doi.org/10.4088/JCP.08m04514
44. Alnawwar, M. A., Alraddadi, M. I., Algethmi, R. A., Salem, G. A., Salem, M. A., & Alharbi, A. A. (2023). The Effect of Physical Activity on Sleep Quality and Sleep Disorder: A Systematic Review. *Cureus, 15*(8), e43595. https://doi.org/10.7759/cureus.43595
45. Sleep Foundation. (n.d.). *ADHD and sleep problems: How are they related?* https://www.sleepfoundation.org/mental-health/adhd-and-sleep
46. Black, D. S., O'Reilly, G. A., Olmstead, R., Breen, E. C., & Irwin, M. R. (2015). Mindfulness meditation and improvement in sleep quality and daytime impairment among older adults with sleep disturbances: A randomized clinical trial. *JAMA Internal Medicine, 175*(4), 494–501. https://doi.org/10.1001/jamainternmed.2014.8081
47. Crawford, N. (2003, February). ADHD: A women's issue. *Monitor on Psychology, 34*(2). https://www.apa.org/monitor/feb03/adhdcounselingwellnesspgh.com+3
48. Cuncic, A. (2024, May 10). *ADHD masking: Examples, impact, and coping.* Verywell Mind. https://www.verywellmind.com/what-is-adhd-masking-5200863
49. Nadeau, K. G. (2023, June). Why ADHD is more challenging for women. *Attention Magazine.* CHADD. https://chadd.org/attention-article/why-adhd-is-more-challenging-for-women/:contentReference{index=1}
50. Bournemouth University. (2023, October 10). *Study reveals connection between ADHD behaviours and technology addictions in adults.* https://www.bournemouth.ac.uk/news/2023-10-10/study-reveals-connection-between-adhd-behaviours-technology-addictions-adults

References

51. Mao, D. M., Danes, S. M., Serido, J., & Shim, S. (2017). Financial influences impacting young adults' relationship satisfaction: Personal management quality, perceived partner behavior, and perceived financial mutuality. *Journal of Financial Therapy, 8*(2), Article 3. https://doi.org/10.4148/1944-9771.1151 New Prairie Press+1

52. Seymour, K. E., Reinblatt, S. P., Benson, L., & Carnell, S. (2015). Overlapping neurobehavioral circuits in ADHD, obesity, and binge eating: evidence from neuroimaging research. *CNS spectrums, 20*(4), 401–411. https://doi.org/10.1017/S1092852915000383

53. Within Health. (2024, May 8). *The relationship between ADHD and binge eating disorder*. https://withinhealth.com/learn/articles/the-relationship-between-adhd-and-binge-eating-disorder

54. Biederman, J., Ball, S. W., Monuteaux, M. C., Surman, C. B., Johnson, J. L., & Zeitlin, S. (2007). Are girls with ADHD at risk for eating disorders? Results from a controlled, five-year prospective study. *Journal of Developmental & Behavioral Pediatrics, 28*(4), 302–307. https://doi.org/10.1097/DBP.0b013e3180327917

55. MacLean, B., Buissink, P., Louw, V., Chen, W., & Richards, T. (2025). Women with symptoms suggestive of ADHD are more likely to report symptoms of iron deficiency and heavy menstrual bleeding. *Nutrients, 17*(5), 785. https://doi.org/10.3390/nu17050785

56. Panossian, A., & Wikman, G. (2010). Effects of Adaptogens on the Central Nervous System and the Molecular Mechanisms Associated with Their Stress-Protective Activity. *Pharmaceuticals (Basel, Switzerland), 3*(1), 188–224. https://doi.org/10.3390/ph3010188

57. Matlen, S. (2022, February 25). *The MTHFR gene mutation: A missing piece of the ADHD genetics puzzle?* ADDitude. https://www.additudemag.com/mthfr-adhd-genetics-puzzle/?srsltid=AfmBOoqjKCG5iZ1fqII2HGpxMJ1HqfEnHvnK6nSYe-AQcZ3nXq9dio3xS

58. Roybal, B., Krueger, A., & Gopal, A. (2023, December 14). *ADHD diet and nutrition: Foods to eat and foods to avoid*. WebMD. https://www.webmd.com/add-adhd/adhd-diets

59. Hovav, K., & Vergnaud, S. (2021, November 17). *How diet and nutrition can affect ADHD*. GoodRx. https://www.goodrx.com/conditions/adhd/diet-and-adhd

60. Griffiths, B. (2023, April 19). *My HRV is very low. Can I increase my heart rate variability?* Polar. https://www.polar.com/blog/my-hrv-is-very-low/ Polar+2

About the Author

Mikaela Salazar is fueled by a deep passion for mental health advocacy, personal development, and helping other women feel seen and understood. With over twenty years of experience as a mental health coach, Mikaela decided to write books on ADHD and other neurodiverse differences to provide women with the tools, insights, and encouragement they need to thrive.

Mikaela understands the frustration of feeling misunderstood and the relief of finally having a roadmap to success and fulfillment. She was diagnosed with ADHD later in life, and she struggled with overwhelm, time management, emotional regulation, and the constant feeling of falling behind, which led her to seek strategies that genuinely work for women juggling multiple roles.

Beyond publishing, Mikaela is an avid hiker, yogi, and reader based on Long Island, New York. She enjoys spending time with her husband, Mark, and their three children in the great outdoors. She is a lifelong learner who always aspires to be a better version of herself and strives to help positively empower others.

www.ingramcontent.com/pod-product-compliance
Lightning Source LLC
Chambersburg PA
CBHW040004040426
42337CB00033B/5218